JOGGING everyone

Charles Williams

and

Clancy Moore

University of Florida
Gainesville, Florida

Hunter Textbooks Inc.

Printed in the United States
Hunter Textbooks Incorporated

ISBN 0-88725-001-7

Cover and cartoons by Deborah Dale

Inquiries should be addressed to the publisher:

▉▉ Hunter Textbooks Inc.

823 Reynolda Road
Winston-Salem, North Carolina 27104

PREFACE

Jogging — Everyone is written in an easy to follow format with specific instructions to help the beginner progress to the advanced stages of jogging. Numerous pictures, illustrations, and charts aid the reader in quickly grasping fitness concepts.

A sixteen-week beginning jogging program divided by fitness categories is provided for those wishing a step-by-step approach. In addition, sixteen lab sessions and a jogging log are included to assist the new jogger in acquiring a better understanding of cardiovascular fitness.

ACKNOWLEDGEMENTS

The authors gratefully acknowledge the following students who posed fo
pictures: Doug Azzarito, Kelly Billings, Michael Caudill, Miguel Carson, Pan
Jordan, Scott Lambert, Mike Neathercliff, Kristen Norris, Maria Poblacki, Marl
Schultheis, Lynn Talerico, and also Peggy Sidman of Robby's Sporting Goods

Grateful acknowledgement should be given to Kelly Billings, Eloise Ellis, and
Linda Williams for typing the manuscript.

Ernestine Godfrey should also be recognized for her handling of editoria
problems which arise in the publishing of any book.

CONTENTS

Chapter 1

Feeling Good About Yourself Through Jogging

In the last ten years jogging has become as much a part of the American way of life as apple pie. Millions of Americans now participate in this natural, simple, and inexpensive physical activity which requires no equipment other than a good pair of running shoes.

When attempting to explain the phenomenal growth of jogging, one must look at the reasons motivating the vast number who participate. Many different personalities with varying levels of fitness comprise that part of the population called "joggers." Since joggers have various needs and desires, it is reasonable to find that people initiate jogging programs for different reasons. This in itself helps to explain the sport's popularity. Not only can jogging satisfy these various needs but, in addition, as one progresses from one level of fitness to another, new needs are formed which are satisfied through the medium of jogging.

Most jogging advocates do not initiate a jogging program to increase heart stroke volume or to increase their ratio of high density lipoprotein. They are primarily interested in the fringe benefits that jogging provides: assisting one in weight loss, firming up muscles, improving general appearance, improving stamina, easing tension, and increasing personal productivity.

High Energy Rx

Some sociologists feel that increasing numbers of Americans are placing less emphasis on material goods and are beginning to search for personal excellence, fulfillment, and contentment, i.e., feeling good about themselves. They are tired of being out of tune with their bodies. They wish to be a perpetual motion machine, bursting with energy, alive and sparkling with wit. As other mortals are winding down, they have visions of just getting started. Perhaps they have discovered that the fittest are really the ones who survive best.

It may be hard to believe, but these individuals are making the right choice. While exercise does require one to expend energy, the returns pay handsome dividends. Many physicians now feel that exercising could be the single most beneficial act to combat fatigue and retard the aging process.

Some people understand and believe in the benefits of regular exercise and, therefore, practice the concepts that lead to attainment. Others may simply need to organize their life-style to include fitness activities in their daily schedule. Still others have either forgotten or have never known the joys of being physically fit. Often during adolescence, habits of inactivity are developed and permitted to become a part of daily living. The continuation of these habits of inactivity is primarily due to the development of labor-saving devices. It has been estimated that more than 95 percent of all movement generated to produce goods is now mechanical rather than human. The invention of the elevator, automobile with power steering and power brakes, riding lawn mower, remote control television and similar devices have made the American people less fit and more lethargic.

It has been said that humans can adjust to anything. This is indeed a fortunate attribute. We do adjust to heat, cold, high altitudes, demanding schedules and to inactivity as well. We are scarcely aware of what happens to our bodies when we become inactive. Such a self-destructive life-style has helped to create one of the most serious epidemics facing mankind.

The 20th Century Plague

Western civilization is in the grip of a modern epidemic. More than 40 million Americans presently have some form of cardiovascular disease. The distinction of being the major cause of death (52 percent) belongs to this category. Another way of stating the problem is that for every American who dies of cancer (the second ranking cause of death), three die of a heart-related illness. Of the deaths attributed to cardiovascular disease, 65 percent are due to heart attacks. While death is difficult to accept at any age, it is particularly tragic when it strikes those who are supposed to be in their prime. Of the deaths in men aged 40-59, forty percent are caused by coronary heart disease. (15)

Essentially, the problem begins with the blood supply to the heart. The heart requires a continuous blood supply which is not supplied by blood being pumped through the heart itself, but is delivered through the coronary arteries. Early in life, deposits of cholesterol and other fatty substances begin to accumulate on the inner walls of the blood vessels. In many cases, the arterial passage narrows to the point that any clot (thrombosis) moving through the bloodstream is quite likely to lodge at this narrowed point. Of course, when this happens the heart muscle in that region quickly dies. Sometimes the blockage is not complete, but the heart muscle blood supply is decreased significantly, causing degrees of chest pain known as angina pectoris.

Medical records indicate that ailments of the heart and blood vessels have increased dramatically during the past decade. Most researchers date the increase as beginning in 1940 when industrialized nations radically reshaped the environment, resulting in a life-style which promoted the risk factors favoring heart disease. Most studies dealing with the identification of factors which seemingly predispose persons to heart disease list the following as most frequently implicated factors: (1) Heredity, (2) Inactivity, (3) Obesity, (4) High blood pressure, (5) Smoking, (6) Stress, (7) High levels of cholesterol, (8) Diabetes, and (9) Sex.

All of the controllable risk factors became more prevalent in the twentieth century. Cigarette smoking, for example, became widespread due to a new technique of flue-curing tobacco. This mild tobacco allowed the fumes to be inhaled into the lungs. Before this time, tobacco had been too offensive to be inhaled. Additionally, mass-production and mass distribution increased availability of the product.

Advanced technology also altered the eating patterns of Americans. Refrigeration and refined techniques of food processing enabled consumers to store foods that were high in fat and cholesterol. Since society was becoming more affluent, the average family could afford a diet previously enjoyed only by the wealthy.

While the primary objective of technical innovations was to eliminate hard physical labor, the human body has not adapted to such a life-style. Physical inactivity is directly related to a mechanized society. We must recognize the fact that regular physical activity is necessary if the body is to function properly. It is somewhat ironic that our ancestors performed physical labor fourteen hours a day and used their leisure time to rest, while our generation makes their living by sitting eight hours a day and must use leisure time for physical exercise.

Eliminating the Heart Attack Horror

Numerous research studies have compared individuals with occupations requiring strenuous physical activity with coworkers who were involved in sedentary positions. (5, 16, 17, 18) Results of these studies show that sedentary workers had an incidence rate of heart attacks from two to four times higher than physically active workers. Also, some of the studies indicated the proportion of men who survived a first attack was more than twice as great among physically active laborers as among those who engaged in sedentary work.

Why do physically active individuals have fewer heart attacks? Scientists now believe that increased efficiency of the heart and lungs from an aerobic training effect (discussed in Chapter 2) is a factor, and also the ratio of cholesterol to high density lipoprotein (HDL). Recent research has established that not all cholesterol is bad, but that one type, HDL, has the capacity to block the formation of cholesterol on the inside of the arteries.

Apparently HDL picks up excess cholesterol from the blood stream and carries it back to the liver for excretion from the body. Excess low density protein on the other hand, appears to be the agent deposited in the linings of the coronary arteries.

Aerobic activities such as jogging increase the amount of good or high density lipoprotein in the blood. One of the more recent studies conducted at Baylor Medical School, has concluded that jogging more than eleven miles per week was associated with a significant increase in blood HDL cholesterol regardless of diet. (7)

From the results of past studies, it is difficult to avoid the conclusion that exercise can decrease the probability of heart attacks. Or, perhaps it seems more fitting to state that the lack of physical activity has a promoting effect on the appearance of heart disease.

Runner's High

Not only do you become healthier from a physiological sense when you jog, but healthier from a psychological standpoint. "I feel more relaxed after I jog," is the most often mentioned benefit by those who practice this form of exercise. While many people begin a jogging program to strengthen their heart or to lose weight, they soon experience interesting changes taking place in their minds. Joggers report an increased ability to adapt to and cope with mental stress, resulting in a more stable and calmer life. The mental processes also seem to be heightened, as joggers indicate they are able to concentrate better and for longer periods of time. They feel more mentally alert and able to think more creatively. All of these psychological side effects contribute to a feeling of greater control over life with a renewed enthusiasm for life itself.

Jogging has been found to be such a powerful antidote to anxiety, depression, and other undesirable mental states that some psychiatrists are prescribing it rather than medication or traditional psychotherapy. Some believe that jogging is the best tranquilizer known. This belief is supported by studies which have shown that fifteen minutes of jogging produces greater relaxation than a normal dose of Valium. (8) Even without a formal structured study, most joggers realize they suffer less from nervous tension, irritability, worry, and sleeplessness as a result of this form of exercise.

The emotional stabilizing effect of jogging and the heightened mental acuity experienced by many is often referred to as "runner's high" or "third wind." The cause of this euphoric state is not fully understood by scientists. They speculate that it may be caused by increased production of the hormone norepinephrine in the brain. After just ten minutes of jogging, production of this hormone is doubled. Or it could be caused by an increased blood flow to the brain. Whatever the cause, jogging can become a "positive addiction" that can increase your mental, as well as physical well-being.

Economic Considerations

In spite of the documented benefits of jogging, there are those who are not motivated by horror stories of future heart attacks and strokes, nor are they enticed with the promise of an euphoric mental state. The attention of such individuals may be obtained only when economic benefits are brought into focus. Such individuals should take notice that the nation's health care bill is over $212 billion or nine percent of the gross national product. (19) The cost of cardiovascular disease alone in 1980 was about $41 billion, including medical services, losses in earnings and production.

The real tragedy is that much of this expense, along with the human suffering, might be avoidable. A study by Purdue University found that the medical costs of a sedentary group was twice the amount spent by a group exercising regularly. (19) A recently completed study by the Prudential Life Insurance Company indicated that employees who participated in a company-sponsored fitness program averaged 3.5 worker disability days as opposed to 8.5 days for those not participating. It was also concluded that if the control group could have reduced its disability days (8.5 per year) to the average of those involved in the fitness program (3.5 per year), the company would have saved $300,000 in salaries alone. (6)

More and more executives are measuring their company's "health" not only by its finances, but also by the health of the people who work for it. Depending on the nature of a company and its product or service, employees directly contribute 50 to 100 percent of its effectiveness.

The economic cost to American industry due to premature deaths is more than 25 billion dollars and 132 million work days of lost time. Heart disease alone accounts for 52 million of those lost days. (3) Industrial leaders are well aware that their companies lose more than sick pay when valued employees are hospitalized in cardiac wards. According to an American Heart Association estimate, recruiting replacements for those who die of heart attack costs industry $700 million every year.

It may be said that healthier employees mean a great deal from two standpoints: theirs and the company's.

Healthy employees:
1. Get more out of their personal and business lives
2. Feel more confident and capable

3. Have a better attitude toward work
4. Are more productive
5. Have a happier home life
6. Have fewer accidents
7. Have less illness
8. Miss fewer days of work
9. Cope with stress better
10. Drink and smoke less

Japanese industry has long recognized the health benefits of physical activity. American corporations are now recognizing the savings of providing a place and time for employees to exercise. Companies such as Xerox, Johnson and Johnson, Phillips Oil, National Cash Register, and Occidental Life Insurance have invested in fitness programs to help their employees take responsibility for and manage their own health. These companies are beginning to realize that, while such programs serve individuals directly, they harvest indirect gains through positive work performance, reduced health costs, increased profits, and positive publicity.

Regardless of the reasons motivating a person to jog, improved health is one result. Increasing the quality and quantity of your life is usually not of concern when you are at an age where you feel you are on top of the world and indestructible. What is needed is a mature, long-term assessment of your life-style and how it will affect your health in twenty or thirty years. As the *Wall Street Journal* put it, "The next major advance in the health of the American people will result only from what the individual is willing to do for himself." This view is upheld by a statement from Roger Egeberg, M.D., Department of HEW, "Fitness can contribute as much to the nation's health (in the future) as immunization and sanitation advances have in the past." (3)

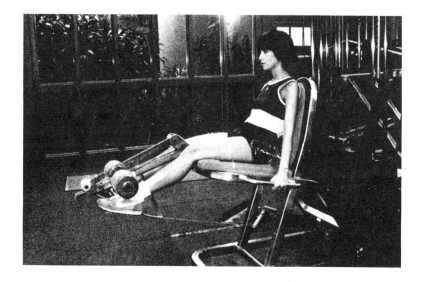

REFERENCES

1. Adner, et al, *Journal of the American Medical Association*, February 8, 1980.

2. Benditt, E., "The Origin of Atherosclerosis." *Scientific American* 236 (2); 74-85, 1977.

3. *Building a Healthier Company.* President's Council on Physical Fitness and Sport. Washington, D.C.

4. Boyer, J.L. and Kasch, F.W., "Exercise Therapy in Hypertensive Men." *Journal of American Medical Association* 211, No. 10 (March 9, 1970) p. 1668.

5. Bruner, D. and Manelis, G., "Physical Activity at Work and Ischemic Heart Disease." In *Coronary Heart Disease and Physical Fitness*, edited by O.A. Larson and R.O. Maimborg. Baltimore: University Park Press, 1971.

6. Cooper, Kenneth A., "Is Physical Fitness Good Business?" *Aerobics,* October 1981, p. 2.

7. Cooper, Kenneth A., "The Cholesterol-HDL Ratio and Physical Fitness." *Aerobics*, September 1981, p. 2.

8. DeVries, Herbert A., "Electromyographic Comparison of Single Doses of Exercise and Meprobamate as to Effects on Muscular Relaxation." *American Journal of Physical Medicine*, Vol. 51, No. 3, 1972.

9. Eshbaugh, Laura, ed., "More Power to You." *Insider*, Fall 1978, pp. 22-23.

10. Fletcher, G.F. and Cantwell, J.D., *Exercise in the Management of Coronary Heart Disease: A Guide for the Practicing Physician.* Springfield, Illinois: C.C. Thomas, 1971.

11. Fisher, A. Garth and Allsen, E. Phillip, *Jogging.* Dubuque, Iowa: Wm. C. Brown, 1980.

12. Fox, S.M. and Haskell, W., "Physical Activity and the Prevention of Coronary Heart Disease." Bulletin of the New York Academy of Medicine, August 1968, p. 950.

13. Frank, C.W., "The Course of Coronary Heart Disease: Factors Relating to Prognosis." Bulletin of the New York Academy of Medicine 44:900, 1968.

14. Gilmore, C.P., *Exercising for Fitness.* Alexandria, Virginia: Time-Life Books, 1981.

15. Miller, David K. and Allen, Earl T., *Fitness: A Lifetime Commitment*, 2nd ed., Minneapolis: Burgess Publishing Company, 1982.

16. Morris, J.N. and Crawford, M.D., "Coronary Heart Disease and Physical Activity of Work." *British Medical Journal* 12:1485, 1958.

17. Morris, J.N. and Crawford, M.D., "Coronary Heart Disease in Transport Workers." *British Journal of Industrial Medicine* 11:260, 1954.

18. Paffenbarger, R.S., et al, "Work Activity of Longshore Men as Related to Death from Coronary Heart Disease and Stroke." *New England Journal of Medicine* 20:1109, 1979.

19. Peters, K., "In America, Corporate Fitness Is an Idea Whose Time Is Now." *Runner's World*, April 1981, pp. 55-59.

20. President's Council on Physical Fitness and Sports Newsletter. Washington, D.C. December 1980, pp. 8-9.

21. Stokes, Roberta; Moore, A.; Moore, C.; and Williams, C. *Fitness: The New Wave.* Winston-Salem, North Carolina: Hunter Textbooks Inc., 1981.

22. Taylor, H.L. "Coronary Heart Disease in Physically Active and Sedentary Populations." *Journal of Sports Medicine and Physical Fitness*, 1962.

23. Zink, V., "At Texas Instruments, Fitness Is Good Business." *Runner's World*, April 1981, p. 58.

Physical fitness means different things to different people. Obviously there is a vast degree of difference in the level and kinds of fitness required by the highly trained athlete, as compared to the average person in our society. You do not have to be an athlete or train like one to be a physically fit person. The object is to train to meet your personal needs.

How do I know if I am physically fit?

You could classify yourself as being physically fit if you are able to work effectively all day; have enough energy remaining at day's end to pursue leisure activities; and have the stamina and strength to meet unexpected physical emergencies. By this definition, a physically fit banker would not require the same physical condition as a physically fit lumberjack.

What about the totality of mind and body?

The relationship between the soundness of body and activities of the mind is subtle and complex. Much is not yet understood, but we do know what the Greeks knew — that intelligence and physical skill can only function at the peak of their capacity when the body is healthy and strong. Physical fitness then is one aspect of total fitness, which includes the social, mental, and emotional makeup of each individual.

What is physical fitness?

Physical fitness is composed of several elements which are usually classified into two groups, **health-related components** and **motor-related components.** Health-related components are those qualities which everyone must have to some degree to be a healthy individual. The components are:

1. **Cardiovascular Endurance**— The ability of the body to persist in strenuous tasks over a prolonged period of time.

2. **Flexibility**— The functional capacity of a joint to move through a normal range of motion. The muscular system is also involved.

3. **Muscular Endurance**— The ability to continue selected muscle group movements for prolonged periods of time.

4. **Muscular Strength**— The ability of a muscle group to contract against a resistance.

Motor-related components are those qualities which enable a person to perform specific motor tasks. They include: coordination, agility, speed, balance, reaction time, and power. Such components are more important to the athlete than to the average person.

Is there any one best sport or activity to promote physical fitness?

No one exercise or sport will develop all of the health-related components on an equal basis. However, aerobic activities that promote cardiovascular endurance are most often identified as having the greatest effect on overall health. This view as expressed in Dr. Kenneth Cooper's book, *The Aerobics Way* (4), touched off the present interest in jogging as much as any single factor. The book was the result of research Dr. Cooper had conducted to find the type of exercise best suited for astronauts who were in training for the Manned Orbiting Laboratory.

How is my level of cardiovascular endurance determined?

Cardiovascular endurance is a measure of the ability of the heart to pump blood, of the lungs to breathe volumes of air, and of the muscles to utilize oxygen. No matter how fit you might appear, if the cardiovascular and respiratory systems cannot meet the demands of sustained activity you will have a low level of fitness. Tests designed to measure cardiovascular endurance, such as the 12 minute run/walk, involve vigorous physical activity that make high demands on the heart and lungs. The maximum oxygen uptake that can be attained measures the effective functioning of the heart, lungs, and vascular system in the delivery of oxygen during periods of work. The higher the maximum oxygen uptake, the more effective the system.

What determines whether an activity is aerobic?

The body's capacity to utilize oxygen can be developed through any aerobic activity. The word *aerobic* means "with oxygen" and involves those activities that can be performed for at least ten minutes without developing an oxygen debt. Examples of such activities include: jogging, swimming, biking, soccer, tennis (singles), and racquetball. For running to be an aerobic activity, it must be performed at a pace whereby oxygen intake accounts for nearly all of the energy expended, or else it could not be maintained for 10 minutes. Anaerobic (without oxygen) running, on the other hand, is a pace which uses oxygen faster than the body can replenish.

If the cardiovascular system is so important, how can I improve mine?

Oxygen is a body fuel most people take for granted. As we now know, the more oxygen the muscles receive, the more energy produced. The oxygen is carried to individual cells by hemoglobin in the blood. Thus, the amount of blood pumped throughout the body correlates with your capacity to do work.

One way to increase your oxygen supply is to exercise the muscle that serves as the pump. Since the heart is a muscle it responds to training as do all other muscles of the body. To develop the heart muscle, you must push it beyond its normal range and make it pump more blood with each beat (stroke volume).

As you begin to jog, the heart beats faster and with greater force causing blood output to be greater with each beat. This increased heart rate is caused by an increased oxygen demand by the muscle cells. During slow-paced jogging, the heart rate reaches a plateau within a few minutes. It will continue at this level until you increase the pace. To maintain a balance between oxygen demand and oxygen supply is therefore the ultimate goal of the cardiovascular system. Fortunately, it is not necessary to exercise at your maximum level to overload the heart. This means that jogging performed at a comfortable pace is a sufficient workload.

What effect does aerobic training have on the heart?

Since a trained heart is stronger and pumps more blood per stroke, it will beat slower than the heart of a more sedentary person. Therefore, fewer beats per minute are necessary to maintain this balance at any given work load (pace).

Several factors influence the amount of blood pumped by the heart:

- One factor is the size of the heart itself. Jogging will increase the total heart volume by increasing the interior dimensions as well as hypertrophy of the heart muscle itself.

- Another factor is the increase in strength of the heart muscle. Jogging will strengthen the heart, enabling it to exert more force. This allows the ventricles to empty almost completely as the blood is forced out.

- A third factor is the amount of blood returning to the heart. When training the heart you should select an activity that is continuous and involves large body muscles. Such activity is desirable because it stimulates the return flow of blood to the heart.

What is the pulse and how do I measure it?

Pulse rate is caused by the pressure of the blood in your body on the arterial walls and corresponds exactly to the beat of the heart. You need to know how to measure your pulse so you can measure the level of intensity and therefore pace yourself properly. Although the pulse can be measured in many different areas of the body, the best spots are at the wrists and neck. Major arteries lie just below the skin at these two locations and can easily be felt by placing your index and middle finger lightly against the skin.

The best spot for measurement is at the base of the thumb in the soft area of the wrist. Care should be taken when counting pulse at the carotid artery of the neck, since pressure exerted against this artery may reduce heart rate and thus yield an inaccurate count.

Practice counting your pulse after you have engaged in different physical activities. Notice how much faster your heart beats, the harder you work. The best way to estimate your heart rate is by counting the pulse for ten seconds immediately after an aerobic task and multiplying by six. Research has shown that the heart rate is nearly the same immediately after jogging (within 10 to 15 seconds) as it is during the activity.

What is resting heart rate?

Research indicates that the rate of your heart beat at rest is an indication of your heart's condition. The best measure of resting heart rate is determined by taking

the pulse for one minute just after waking in the morning, while in the lying position. The American Heart Association identifies the normal range for resting heart rate as between 50-100. However, research shows that persons with resting heart rates over 70 have a much greater risk of heart attack than those with rates below 70, and that the risk increases proportionally above or below 70. (6) In addition, we know that those who develop high levels of cardiovascular endurance often have resting heart rates below 50 beats per minute. The resting pulse rate will gradually decrease in response to a jogging program. By keeping a record of your resting pulse rate, you can measure the progress being achieved.

What is blood pressure and why is it important?

If you had a physical examination, your blood pressure was probably checked. Blood pressure is recorded in two numbers and is measured in millimeters of mercury. The first number recorded is called the systolic pressure and is your blood pressure at the moment blood is pumped from the heart. The second number is the diastolic pressure and represents the blood pressure between beats when the heart is relaxed. The optimal range for your blood pressure is stated as:

$$\frac{120 \pm 20}{80 \pm 10}$$

Generally blood pressure rises with either an increase in cardiac output or with an increase in resistance to blood flow.

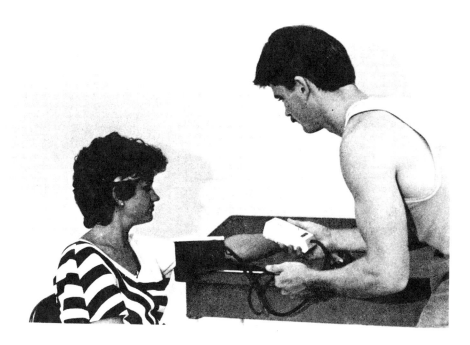

Of course, physical activity requires your heart to pump more blood, thus a poor physical condition may cause a sharp rise in both systolic and diastolic pressure. As physical fitness improves there will be a smaller rise in blood pressure. As a matter of fact, highly trained endurance athletes may have no significant increase in diastolic pressure or it may be a little lower during sustained vigorous exercise. (13)

Systolic pressure may go up and down within a limited range during exercise. If your blood pressure starts high and stays high during rest, it is called hypertension. Many people with moderately elevated blood pressure can significantly lower this pressure by altering their life-style. In any case, you should definitely know what your blood pressure is, the factors affecting it, and what you can do to control it.

Specifically what changes will jogging have on my cardiovascular system?

Jogging conducted in a proper manner results in:

- A longer resting phase of heart cycle which enables the heart to have a more complete filling of the chambers, resulting in the myocardium receiving proper nutrients and expediting removal of waste products. (The heart does not receive blood until relaxed; therefore, the longer the rest, the better.)

- A hypertrophy of the heart muscle which ultimately results in a stronger heart.

- An increased contractility of the heart muscle.

- An increased stroke volume enabling more blood to be pumped with each stroke. This improves the ability to transport more rapidly life-sustaining oxygen from the lungs to the heart and ultimately to all parts of the body.

- An increase in cardiac output (minute volume).

- An increase in blood volume — a temporary anemia may occur as a result of this change and a fragmentation of red blood cells during heavy training.

- Venous return is increased due to "muscle pump."

- An increase in red blood cells.

- An increase in hemoglobin.

- Lactic acid formation is lessened due to an increase in oxygen supply.

- An increase in white cells following muscular work.

- An increase in blood pressure during exercise is less in the trained individual.

- An increase in buffering capacity of the blood.

- A lowering in blood pressure.
- An increase in high density lipoprotein ratio.

RESPIRATORY SYSTEM

What role does the respiratory system play in developing physical fitness?

Obviously you're getting enough oxygen to live on, but increasing your oxygen intake makes the body organs work better and increases energy. Since the body cells are not in direct contact with the external environment, the respiratory system plays a vital role in the functioning of the body and especially in its ability to produce a high energy output.

Breathing is, of course, the process of external respiration by which oxygen in the air is brought into the lungs and into close contact with the blood which absorbs it and carries it to all parts of the body. The oxygen intake is dependent upon the maintenance of a free airway and the proper diffusion of gas to the cells throughout the body. This phase is critical because any abnormality which impairs the proper passage of air to the lungs will disturb the gas diffusion, and consequently leave arterial blood with insufficient quantities of oxygen and, at the same time, fail to rid the circulatory system of carbon dioxide.

As air enters the lungs, hemoglobin in the blood flows through capillaries imbedded in the walls of the alveoli exchanging oxygen and carbon dioxide. In normal situations, the blood is about 98 percent saturated with oxygen when it leaves the lungs. When at rest, about 30 percent of this oxygen is removed at the cellular level, but during heavy exercise this value can be increased almost three times. Oxygen uptake is the amount of oxygen extracted from the circulating blood in one minute and, when measured during maximal exercise, it is termed **maximum oxygen uptake**. Because maximal oxygen uptake represents the ability of the body to mobilize all its systems during physical stress, it is considered the best single indication of one's level of physical fitness. (14)

Since the lungs have the ability to respond and are capable of providing more than enough oxygen, the respiratory system is exceptionally responsive to the oxygen needs of the body. Therefore, the failure to meet increasing oxygen demands during physical activity (short of breath) is due to blood supply and not respiration.

Will jogging improve my respiratory system?

Yes, jogging can accomplish the following:

- Greater chest expansion.
- The depth of the chest is increased.

- Breathing rate in the trained individual is slower at rest.

- An increase in alveolar air space.

- Blood is exposed to oxygen over a greater area.

- The muscles of respiration are strengthened and consequently there is a reduction in resistance to air flow which ultimately facilitates the rapid flow of air in and out of the lungs.

- In performing similar work, a trained individual takes in smaller amounts of air and absorbs oxygen from the air in greater amounts than an individual not in training. It is believed that the increased number of capillaries in the lungs and an increase in alveolar air space, resulting in more blood being exposed to more air at any given time, are responsible for this economy in respiration.

MUSCULAR SYSTEM

How are muscles dependent on oxygen?

Very simply, a muscle can be described as a band of contractile fibers held together by a sheath of connective tissue. Muscles attach to bones by means of tendons which stem from the connective tissue sheath. Ligaments are like tendons, but ligament fibers will stretch and join bone to bone instead of muscle to bone.

When performing work, especially that of a continuous nature such as jogging, the muscles demand a steady supply of oxygen to continue production of energy. The amount of work which one can perform and how long it can be continued are dependent on the amount of oxygen which can be consumed and, therefore, the amount of energy which can be created.

All movements of the body depend on the functioning — contraction and relaxation — of muscle tissue. Although your cardiovascular system may be able to deliver large quantities of oxygen to the muscles, this will not insure that the oxygen will be utilized. In addition to the functioning of the delivery system, the ability of the muscles to absorb oxygen from the blood in sufficient quantity is important.

The absorption of oxygen from the blood into muscle cells is made possible by the presence of a substance within the cells called **myoglobin.** Myoglobin is an iron-containing protein similar to hemoglobin. It is also responsible for the storage of oxygen within the muscle cells. Once absorbed into myoglobin, the oxygen combines with nutrients (fats and carbohydrates) and enters the mitochondria of the muscle fibers. Mitochondria are tiny structures within the muscle fibers where oxygen and chemical substances are brought together to produce a series of chemical reactions which provide most of the energy required for muscular endurance activities.

Will jogging improve my muscular system?

Proper jogging improves the muscular system in the following ways:

- Increased muscle size (greater cross-section area). It is believed that muscle fibers increase in size but do not increase in number. This relates directly to strength.

- Proliferation of capillaries. The result is a better circulation of blood to the muscles and an increase in muscular endurance.

- The sarcolemma of the muscle fibers becomes thicker and stronger.

- The amount of connective tissue within the muscle thickens.

- Nerve impulses travel more readily across the motor end plate.

- In summary, the muscle becomes stronger, increases in endurance, reacts more quickly and efficiently, and is less prone to injury.

REFERENCES

1. American Medical Association. *The Wonderful Human Machine*. Chicago, 1971.

2. American Heart Association, *Facts About Heart and Blood Vessel Disease*, 1975.

3. Clarke, David H. *Exercise Physiology*. Englewood Cliffs, New Jersey: Prentice-Hall, 1975.

4. Cooper, Kenneth A. *The Aerobics Way*. Bantam Books, 1978.

5. DeVries, Herbert A. *Physiology of Exercise*. Dubuque, Iowa: Wm. C. Brown, 1970.

6. Elrick, Harold; Crakes, James; and Clarke, Sam. *Living Longer and Better*. Mountain View, California: World Publications, 1978.

7. Eshbaugh, Laura, ed. "The New Fitness: Focus on Personal Energy." *Insider*, Fall 1978, p. 7.

8. Falls, Harold; Baylor, Ann; and Dishman, Rod. *Essentials of Fitness*. Philadelphia: Saunders College, 1980.

9. Fisher, A. Garth and Allsen, E. Phillip. *Jogging*. Dubuque, Iowa: Wm. C. Brown, 1980.

10. Fisher, A. Garth and Conlee, Robert. *The Complete Book of Physical Fitness*. Salt Lake City: Brigham Young University Press, 1979.

11. MacLennan, Douglas. *The Fitness Institute Bulletin*, Vol. 3, No. 1, 1980.

12. MacLennan, Douglas, ed. *The Fitness Institute Bulletin*, Vol. 3, No. 4, April 1980.

13. Miller, David and Allen, Earl. *Fitness: A Lifetime Commitment*. Minneapolis: Burgess Publishing Company, 1979.

14. Stokes, Roberta; Moore, A.; Moore, C.; and Williams, C. *Fitness: The New Wave*. Winston-Salem, North Carolina: Hunter Textbooks Inc., 1981.

15. Wilmore, Jack H. "Maximal Oxygen Intake and Its Relationship to Endurance Capacity on a Bicycle Ergometer." *Research Quarterly* 40 (March 1969), p. 203.

Chapter 3
Questions Most
Often Asked
About Jogging

Should everyone jog?

No. Jogging may aggravate a physical defect or old injuries in some people. If so, they should go to an aerobic activity that is gravity supporting, such as cycling or swimming. Also, some feel jogging is boring. If you don't like it, don't force yourself to do it.

What about joggers dying from enlarged hearts?

While some victims of heart failure do have large hearts just as long distance runners do, their similarity ends sharply. In most heart failure patients, the muscle fibers only appear to be large because they are swollen with fluid. Distance runners have heart muscle fibers that are strong and large.

Is there any truth to the contention that kidneys and other internal organs can be damaged from the constant jarring produced by jogging?

There is no evidence that jogging per se can cause this kind of damage. However, severe dehydration which can be brought on by jogging in very hot and humid weather could cause severe kidney damage. This type of problem is very rare among joggers.

I have heard that female joggers have a hard time getting pregnant. Is this true?

Research has indicated that the excessive loss of body fat does affect ovulation in females. Therefore, it is quite possible that jogging thirty or more miles a week might cause ovulation to become infrequent or cease altogether.

While jogging last week I acquired a pain in the center of my chest. Is this normal?

No, it is not. Pain should always be regarded as a red light in any exercise program.

Is there any truth to the contention that jogging conditions the heart but ages the face?

When joggers appear to have advanced facial aging, invariably the cause is not jogging per se, but the sun and wind. To reduce exposure to the elements, try wearing a hat, using sunscreen, and jogging in the early morning or late evening.

Is it true that taking "No Doz" tablets before jogging could trigger a case of heatstroke?

"No Doz" tablets are basically caffeine, and caffeine given to a susceptible person, operating in high temperature, can elevate body temperature to a critical level.

Can jogging help a person suffering from migraine headaches?

Many doctors are now prescribing jogging in lieu of medication for this problem, and have experienced an astonishing number of "cures."

My problem is weak ankles. What can I do to strengthen them?

There are many excellent exercises, but one of the easiest and best is to cut a ring of rubber from an old rubber tube. Now slip your toes of both feet inside the ring, and holding your heels together attempt to spread your feet apart.

One of my feet is smaller than the other. What should I do?

Some serious joggers buy two different sized shoes. However, a piece of sponge or felt under the shoe tongue will prevent the smaller foot from sliding. Some people also wear a heavier sock on the smaller foot.

What do you think about running in "ankle weights"?

Not much. The additional weight may change your stride which in turn may cause other problems. Increased conditioning is best served by either running farther, faster, or both.

What is Morton's toe?

Morton's toe is characterized by a second toe that is longer than the other toes. When buying shoes be certain to leave at least one inch of space between the longest toe and the tip of your shoe. Joggers with this problem frequently consult a good sport podiatrist for help.

I like to jog, but almost always get blisters. Is there anything I can do to prevent this?

A blister is caused by excessive friction. Non-fitting shoes, rapidly increasing mileage, or an abnormal gait also can cause blisters. Try buying your shoes late in the day when your feet are swollen and make sure that the shoe matches the shape of your foot. Lubrication or foot powder on your feet and in your shoes also help.

My running shoes are really beginning to smell. Is there anything that can be done?

Two things are likely to cause smelly shoes: one is the possibility of athlete's foot and the other is that the uppers of your shoes may not be permeable to water. Place shoes in a well ventilated area for drying, wear clean absorbent socks and restrict wear to jogging.

My running shoes wear very quickly. Is there anything that I can do to save money and keep from buying new shoes so frequently?

Other than perhaps buying a shoe with a tougher sole, shoe glue is about the only solution. When applying, however, be sure you build the surface only to its original level. An uneven surface on the sole of a shoe can cause real problems.

Would training in a rubber suit make me a tougher runner?

No, but it could very well kill you. The problem is that the body heats up much faster and, with no means of cooling by sweat evaporation, you are in serious trouble. It is imperative that the body have an opportunity to cool itself by sweat evaporation.

How many calories can I burn by jogging one mile?

You will burn one calorie per kilogram (2.2 lbs.) of body weight for every kilometer (.62 of a mile) which you jog. This extrapolates out to about 100 calories per mile.

Is fructose (fruit sugar) better for a jogger than table sugar?

Like all complex sugars, fructose is converted by the liver into glucose. The basic difference is that fruits contain fiber which in turn holds the sugar in the intestines for a longer length of time. This, of course, will cause your body blood sugar level to rise more slowly.

If I take sugar while jogging will it increase my endurance?

Yes, if you run long enough for the extra sugar to get into the blood stream for absorption by your muscles. However, if you are adequately trained you should have enough sugar in your muscles for races up to 20 miles. A top marathon runner can usually go the distance without adding sugar.

Is honey more healthful than granulated sugar?

No, both end up doing the same thing for your body.

Why should joggers not drink milk?

This is true for only some joggers. Some people lack a chemical in their intestines which allows the body to break down the "double sugar" in milk to a single component. Because the body cannot absorb a double sugar, it moves into the lower intestine where bacteria ferment it, causing gas.

Will eating large amounts of protein make me stronger?

No. The only way to make your muscles larger and stronger is to exercise against resistance.

Can I hurt myself by taking in large amounts of protein?

Since your body has no way to store excessive protein, your liver and kidneys are forced into working much harder. Studies using rats have determined that this practice may cause an enlargement of kidneys and liver. Another undesirable side effect created by unnecessary protein is the creation of extra ammonia and organic acids which act as a diuretic causing you to lose fluids excessively. This can ultimately cause dehydration, increasing the potential for heat stroke if exercising in hot weather.

I am confused as to how much I should drink during prolonged exercise in hot weather. What do you suggest?

Two to three quarts of water are consumed by the average person each day. Much more is needed by joggers, especially if they exercise in hot weather. Athletes used to believe it was bad to drink during a workout. Studies have shown this to be untrue. Fluids should be replaced as soon as they are lost. Most authorities recommend drinking before you jog to compensate in advance for fluid losses.

There are a number of "special drinks" on the market. Which is best?

One 1978 study compared Gatorade, Body Punch, Water, and Braketime for carbohydrate contribution and gastric emptying time. The report indicated that Braketime, Body Punch, and Water cleared the stomach much more quickly than Gatorade. Both Braketime and Body Punch contain the most carbohydrates and have less than 2.5 percent sugar.

I sometimes get a sharp pain in the side while jogging. How can this be avoided?

The common term for this is "stitch." There is no hard and fast rule for its cause. Most experts feel the cause may be due to a lack of oxygen, eating before jogging, or an inability to relax. The problem disappears with increased conditioning.

Can I jog during my menstrual period?

Research indicates that exercise helps to reduce menstrual discomforts. Female athletes tend to have less menstrual problems than women who exercise little.

Does jogging produce or contribute to varicose veins?

There are few runners who have varicose veins. What is not known is whether running has a beneficial effect or whether people who have varicose veins do not run. We do know that muscular action plays a significant role in the blood exchange process in the leg. Running enhances the return flow of blood from the legs.

When I run seriously for time my arms seem to tighten up and become very heavy. What would you suggest?

Light weight work seems to be the order of the day for you. Try doing presses and curls, two or three times a week, using five to ten pound weights. Running hills also will strengthen arms and upper body.

I frequently see the word "Fartlek." What does it mean?

It is a Swedish word meaning "speed play." This training technique first became popular in the 1940s and consists essentially of sprinting until you are out of breath, then jogging or walking to recover, then repeating again.

If I go to the mountains this summer, will it affect my jogging performance?

As long as you are running below 3000 feet elevation you will notice little or no difference. Above 3000 feet will cause a decrease in performance. It usually takes four to six weeks to adjust.

How will I know if I am jogging too much?

Your body will tell you. Excessive pain is always the prime indicator.

I like to jog, but unfortunately am growing older. What can I expect in terms of losing my physical abilities?

Barring major illness or other complications you can expect the following:

1. Maximum work capacity (VO_2 MAX) peaks at about 20 years of age and gradually declines each year. If you make it to age 65, your capacity will be about 70 percent of a 25-year-old person. However, there are some 65-year-olds who have a higher VO_2 MAX than a much younger untrained person.

2. The amount of body fat on 65-year-old joggers is significantly less than that of 65-year-old nonjoggers.

3. Maximum heart rate decreases about one beat per year after age 20. This is an average.

In the initial stages, what's more important, the speed or how long you jog?

When you first start out, duration and frequency of the activity is most important. Go at a pace you can maintain for at least twenty minutes, three times a week. For some, this may mean walking. While it is necessary to implement the overload principle, you must remember to "**train and not strain**." As your endurance increases, you can then start increasing the pace (intensity).

How much must I jog to acquire all the benefits that an aerobic activity provides?

Most authorities agree that jogging two miles per day, three days a week (frequency) is sufficient. However, to increase the level of HDL, a 12-mile total per week is recommended. To receive all of the benefits research has shown jogging can provide, the distance must be at a pace that will elevate heart rate to 70-85 percent (intensity) of maximum for 20-30 minutes (duration).

What is the best surface to jog on?

Unquestionably, a smooth grass or dirt surface is the most absorbant, thereby causing fewer feet, leg, knee, hip and back injuries.

My high school physical education teacher never stressed a cool-down. How do I go about it?

You should gradually decrease your pace to a walk until the pulse rate lowers to 100-120 beats per minute. The next phase of your cool-down should involve some of the same stretching exercises you did in the warm-up. The entire process could last from 5 to 10 minutes.

What exercise should I do besides jogging?

When jogging, the muscles in the back of the leg become stronger and shorter than those in the front. With such a muscle imbalance, it becomes important to engage in exercises that stretch the muscles in the back of the leg and strengthen those in the front, i.e., quadriceps. Riding a bicycle is excellent.

At what rate will jogging help me lose weight?

Research has shown the major cause of obesity is inactivity. If food intake remained constant, you could lose 20-30 pounds a year by jogging. It is possible to decrease percentage of body fat, but gain weight during a conditioning program since muscles weigh more than fat. You should be more concerned about your percentage of body fat than with body weight.

Chapter 4
Training Principles

When you decide to start a jogging program, remember your initial performance should match your degree of present condition. After all, if it took you several years to get out of shape it's going to take you more than 10 days to get back into shape.

A sound jogging program is one developed on an individual basis, taking into consideration individual differences in age, resting heart rate, and previous involvement in physical activity. The foundation for selection of a point of departure within an individualized jogging program is the result of the testing program. Once cardiovascular tests have been administered, specific training concepts can then be applied.

The term *training* refers to the systematic procedure in which a person prepares to perform strenuous work in an efficient manner and to recuperate from that work as quickly as possible. The main objective of any cardiovascular fitness program is to increase the body's ability to utilize oxygen within a controlled time span. This is a complex procedure, involving the heart, lungs, blood, and blood vessels. Therefore, the physical activity that is selected to strengthen the heart and lungs requires a carefully planned and deliberate training program.

The following principles of training are the result of considerable research. Following these guidelines will enable you to operate efficiently while avoiding excessive strain and possible injury.

Adaptation

Adaptation refers to the body's ability to adjust to stress. This means that as you force your body to work harder, it will eventually adapt so as to work more efficiently.

Overload

Overload occurs when exercise is increased, thus placing increased demands on the body. The body adapts to the increased workload after a period of time. Overload is accomplished in three ways: **intensity, duration,** and **frequency.**

1. Intensity:

The intensity of a training program requires that the exercise be vigorous enough to demand more effort than usual. One must strive to place a repeatedly greater than normal workload on the body until it has adapted to the increased demand. For jogging this means you must make your heart work harder than it normally does. How much harder is a critical question. Overly-strenuous exercise may cause extreme discomfort, while not training vigorously enough will result in little or no improvement.

Each person has a maximum heart rate which should not be exceeded, regardless of the demands placed on it. The major factor limiting maximum heart rate is age. The older you become, the lower your maximum heart rate. The greatest cardiovascular benefits result from exercises that are vigorous enough to make your heart rate increase 70 to 85 percent of your maximum. Jogging at a faster pace, making the heart exceed 85 percent of your maximum rate, quickly brings on fatigue without noticeable improvements.

The 70 to 85 percent range is termed the target zone and is the desired level of intensity for most people. Not everyone, however, will be able to jog vigorously enough in the beginning to bring their heart rate into the target zone. If you have not exercised for some time or are extremely overweight, you should not go to the full overload. Instead, begin at a lighter load, i.e., a 50 percent working rate, and gradually progress toward the 70 to 85 percent range.

To compute *your* target zone, you must first determine your own maximum heart rate. This can be done precisely during a stress test using elaborate laboratory equipment. A less expensive approximation that is accurate enough for training purposes can be accomplished by subtracting your age from 220. The resting pulse rate is subtracted from your maximum heart rate. This value is multiplied by percent of maximum you wish to train and then added to the resting pulse.

220 − age − resting pulse × 70 percent + resting pulse = target zone

The target zone enables you to check the intensity of your exercise by stopping briefly from time to time to monitor your pulse rate. If your pulse falls below the target zone, speed up your pace; if it goes above, decrease the pace. Basically, the speed at which you must walk or jog to reach your target zone depends on how fit you are. As you increase your fitness level, additional overload will be required to keep your heart rate in the target zone.

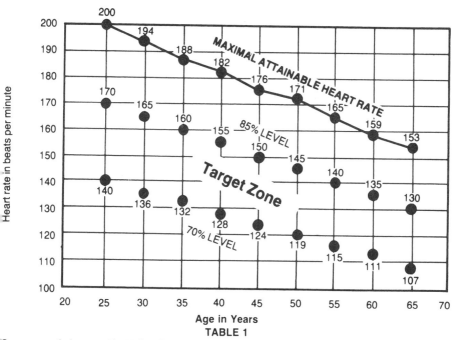

TABLE 1

Summary of changes that take place as a result of age as far as the maximal attainable heart rate is concerned and what the target zone is for each age group. The numerical values shown are "average" values for each age. (Courtesy Best Foods Division, CPC International, Englewood Cliffs, N.J.)

One helpful hint in monitoring your pulse while jogging is to compute your target zone at 50, 60, 70, 80, and 85 percent, then divide each by 6. This will provide you with a 10-second target heart rate and eliminate the palm as a scratch pad. For example, if your target zone for 70 percent is 162, you would divide by 6 and arrive at a 10 second target heart rate of 27. If after five minutes of jogging you counted 24 pulse beats in 10 seconds, you would know to slightly increase the intensity of your jog, by about 10 percent.

2. Duration:

The duration of the exercise refers to the length of each training session. In order to be effective, an exercise must be maintained for a significant length of time. For jogging, this means maintaining the target heart rate for 20 to 30 minutes to achieve the training effect. Research shows that as duration is increased, intensity will decrease. This inversed relationship may determine for you whether you increase your pace or distance travelled. For example, if you were unable to maintain a pace for 45 minutes that would keep your pulse in the target zone, the distance would have to be shortened. On the other hand, if after jogging a few

Choose an overload to suit your individual needs.

Monitoring your pulse.

weeks for 30 minutes each work session you were steadily increasing your pace to keep your pulse in the target zone, you may elect to increase your distance (duration).

Regardless of the intensity, the effectiveness of the exercise increases as the duration increases. Forty-five minutes of jogging is better than 30, and 30 is better than 20 minutes. Duration beyond one hour is not recommended for the value derived unless one is training for competition. Dr. Kenneth Cooper believes that

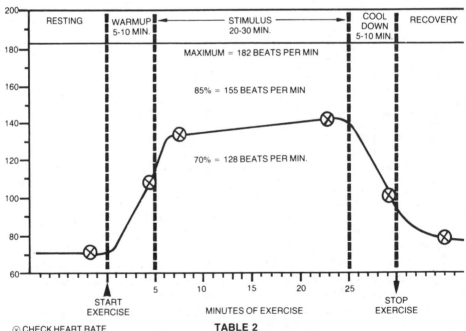

⊗ CHECK HEART RATE

TABLE 2
THE EXERCISE TRAINING PATTERN

jogging more than 15 miles a week yields diminishing returns. Cooper's studies show that jogging 11 miles a week satisfies most of the requirements for cardiovascular development and that jogging more than 15 miles greatly increases the chance of injury. Anything less than 15 to 20 minutes will not provide all the benefits possible. Yet for the beginner it may be necessary to start with less time and progressively apply the overload principle and increase the duration of the exercise session.

3. Frequency:

The principle of frequency refers to the fact that jogging must be performed regularly if you are to reach an adequate level of cardiovascular fitness. Ideally, your jogging program will be a part of your daily life-style; however, benefits can be achieved with fewer workouts. Research indicates that three workouts per week on alternate days can produce results if the duration of each workout is increased by five or ten minutes over the time worked out on four days. The beginning jogger may elect to start jogging three days per week, then increase the overload by jogging four days, then five days, and finally on a daily basis. Jogging two days per week is not acceptable for cardiovascular improvement, although such a jogging schedule may maintain the level you have acquired.

Progression. Progression is a combination of adaptation and overload. Since the body adjusts to stress, the amount of work must be periodically increased in order for improvement to occur. For example, if you begin an exercise program that involves running one mile a day in eight minutes you would probably find the workout stressful. You would, therefore, improve your cardiovascular function for the next several weeks if you continued the eight minute rate. But, if you continued to perform at that level, i.e., run the same distance in the same time, cardiovascular improvement would stop and adaptation would occur. To continue improving, you would have to increase your stress by running a mile in seven minutes. That would place additional stress on your cardiovascular system and, therefore, the overload principle would again go into effect. In a few weeks or months, additional overload would have to be added.

It is extremely important that a person frequently monitor the recovery heart rate to determine when it is safe to progress. The guiding principle is that **5 - 6 minutes after the workout your heart rate should return to about 120 beats per minute, and after 10 minutes should drop to less than 100 beats per minute.**

Specificity. The principle of specificity implies that the improvements made in training are specific to the type of training undertaken. For example, a strength program will develop strength, but not an appreciable amount of cardiovascular endurance. Another illustration is the person who has adequately trained for a sport such as swimming, but when that person participates in basketball or some other sport, he or she quickly becomes fatigued during play and muscle sore later.

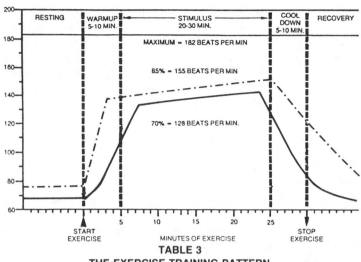

TABLE 3
THE EXERCISE TRAINING PATTERN

Comparison of an untrained individual's heart rate to that of one who is physically fit. Even though both are performing the same task, note how the untrained person's heart rate is higher to begin with and shows a sharp increase to the slightest amount of exertion. Additionally, heart rate recovery period is much longer for the untrained person.

Each activity requires specific demands, and doing the event is the best way to train for the event.

Retrogression. When following a training program, you may find that at certain levels in the program you reach a plateau or seem to slightly decrease in performance. Try as you may, it seems you are unable to regain or surpass your previous level. Then suddenly, for no apparent reason, you may surge ahead surpassing all previous levels. The reasons for such retrogression are not clear except that the body may be making adjustments to meet the demands of the overload. When the adjustments are effected, then the progress or improvement is made.

Use and Disuse. Use and disuse, simply stated, means that if you train, there will be improvement. If not, physical performance will decline. Use stimulates the function of the organism, and disuse results in deterioration.

Muscle Recruitment. The ability of the body to call upon additional muscle units is dependent upon the individual's level of training. Thus, if the load or task is slight, a few units are stimulated, and if the load is heavy, many units are stimulated or "recruited."

Skill. Improvement in muscle usage facilitates improvement in skill, which in turn improves physical performance and results in improved coordination.

Individual Rates of Response. Each person will have his or her own level of response to a jogging program. Many people who train or participate on athletic teams seem to arrive at a high level of condition long before others. The reason is probably dependent upon many factors, some of which are emotional and others that are hereditary. A few of the variables may be: (1) present physical condition; (2) age; (3) body type; (4) weight; (5) rest, sleep and relaxation; (6) nutrition; (7) freedom from disease; (8) motivation; and (9) ability to learn new skills.

INTERVAL TRAINING

While most people agree that running or jogging long, slow distances is an excellent means of improving cardiovascular endurance, another method called interval training has also gained wide-spread acceptance.

The chief differences between the two systems are the length of work periods and the degree of intensity. A common interval workout usually consists of three to seven work periods of three to five minutes duration, at about 85 percent maximum capacity. These periods of work are broken by short rest periods of walking or jogging to partially recover for the next work period. The length of the rest or recovery period is usually based on a heart rate recovery plan, with 120 beats per minute classified as minimal. That is, if your heart rate reaches 160 during the exercise bout, you must jog or walk until your heart rate drops to 120 beats per minute. As your system becomes more efficient, your recovery rate time will decrease.

The advantages of interval training over continuous training appear to be the following:

1. More work can be accomplished in less time.

2. Greater flexibility in the work program reduces boredom.

3. Because of the short work periods, the intensity of the work can be greater.

The requirements or possible disadvantages seem to be the following:

1. Length of the rest period must be no greater than 1 to 3. A more acceptable ratio of work to relief period is 1 to 2 or 1 to 1.

2. If aerobic power is the objective, then the length of the work period must be at least 3 - 5 minutes.

3. The heart rate intensity must be 70 to 85 percent of maximum.

Overload for this system of training can be achieved or increased by:

1. Reducing the length of the recovery period

2. Increasing the intensity of the work period

3. Increasing the number of work periods

4. Increasing the length of the work period

5. Any combination of the above

JOGGING — A PART OF YOUR DAILY ROUTINE

The best way to keep from falling into the all-too-common syndrome of having a one-day layoff turn into two, then into three, and so on until you stop jogging altogether, is to make your workout a part of your daily routine. Schedule time for yourself and, regardless of what comes up, take that time for your daily jog. After all, you are important and so is your health.

Some individuals have started successful jogging programs by alternating a day of jogging with a day of walking. Since we are a creature of habit, you are more likely to stay with a fitness program if you reserve the same time slot each day for your exercise. In fact, you may feel something is missing without your daily activity.

When Is the Best Time to Jog?

The time you select is up to you. Consider whether you are a morning or an evening person, when you function best, and when there is least demand for your time. The effects are the same, whether you jog morning, noon, or evening, except for the temperature or possibly wind. You may elect to run in the morning during summer months since it is cooler and at noon or in the afternoon during winter months. The following advantages and disadvantages for each time period may also be considered.

Morning Jogging

Advantages:

1. Wakes you up for the day's activities

2. Traffic is usually light

3. Cool and clean air — those with allergies should consider this time

4. Very unlikely that other people or activities would interfere with this schedule

Disadvantages:

1. Dark and cold for a large part of the year

2. You're less limber at this time of day

3. If you're not a morning person, it's hard to roll out of bed and go straight into an exercise program.

One research study found that morning joggers stayed with the activity more than those who ran later in the day. However, morning joggers suffered more injuries.

Noon Jogging

Advantages:

1. Neither sleepy or drowsy

2. Few social obligations

3. Provides physical break from mental fatigue

Disadvantages:

1. Finding a convenient jogging route near place of work

2. Finding a dressing and shower facility

Evening Jogging

Advantages:

1. Usually one feels more flexible

2. Has tendency to calm you down after facing the day's problems

3. Easier to find others to jog with

Disadvantages:

1. Demand for your time from work and family obligations

2. Early darkness during winter months

3. Sometimes hard to motivate yourself to go out and overload your system after completing a hard day's work

MAINTAINING A JOGGING LOG

An easy method to keep records of your progress is to maintain a jogging log. The log has many advantages that make it worth the small amount of time required to write down the information:

1. You should not depend on your memory for distance covered, time elapsed, etc. It is far better to have an objective measurement written down to guide you in your progress.

2. Some individuals need written evidence to keep them honest about their jogging. Running stories tend to be more exaggerated than fishing tales.

3. It is a good source of information for setting goals, planning a program, avoiding injury and determining peak performance periods.

Most successful people use a data base to make decisions. Likewise, one can hardly be a knowledgeable jogger without information regarding daily progress.

Jogging logs or diaries come in many forms. Information that should be recorded in your daily log includes the date, distance covered, time required, exercise heart rate, resting heart rate, distance for week, and cumulative distance since program was begun. Appendix B provides forms for one such log.

JOGGING LOG

Name _Jane Doe_ _____ Section _4321_ Date _1-6-83_

	Date	Resting H.R.	Exercise H.R.	Time	Distance	Total Week	Total Year	Comments
M	1-10	72	161	12 min.	1 mile	1 mile	1 mile	Tired legs and feet okay.
T	1-11	70	164	11:48	1	2	2	Calves sore
W	1-12	71	158	10:15	1	3	3	additional stretches help
T	1-13	—	160	13:15	1.13	4.13	4.13	little stiffness
F	1-14	—	165	13:00	1.13	5.26	5.26	very loose
S	1-15	69	170	11:15	1.13	6.39	6.39	right toe blister
S	1-16							
M	1-17	71	167	15:00	1.25	1.25	7.64	toe getting better
T	1-18	—	174	12:30	1.25	2.50	8.89	couldn't get going
W	1-19	70	170	12:30	1.25	3.75	10.14	lack endurance
T	1-20							
F	1-21	70	164	12:10	1.25	5.00	11.39	easy run
S	1-22	—	169	15:20	1.38	6.38	12.77	new stretches help
S	1-23	69	171	14:50	1.38	7.76	14.15	cold
M	1-24	69	168	13:40	1.50	1.50	15.65	need to relax more
T	1-25	—	165	14:10	1.50	3.00	16.75	gaining endurance
W	1-26	68	162	14:00	1.50	4.50	18.25	feeling good
T	1-27	69	170	17:20	1.75	6.25	20.00	enjoying it
F	1-28	—	167	17:40	1.75	8.00	21.75	sleeping better
S	1-29							
S	1-30	68	162	17:30	1.75	9.75	23.50	why didn't I do this before

REFERENCES

1. Corbin, C. B.; Dowell, L. J.; and Tolson, H. *Concepts in Physical Education.* Dubuque, Iowa: Wm. C. Brown, 1974.

2. Cundiff, D. and Brunteson, P. *Health Fitness: A Guide to a Lifestyle.* Dubuque, Iowa: Kendall/Hunt Company, 1979.

3. Editors of *Runner's World. The Complete Runner.* Mountain View, California: World Publications, 1974.

4. Fisher, A. Garth and Allsen, E. Phillip. *Jogging.* Dubuque, Iowa: Wm. C. Brown, 1980.

5. Henderson, Joe. *Jog, Run, Race.* Mountain View, California: World Publications, 1977.

6. Hockey, R. *Physical Fitness: The Pathway to Healthful Living.* St. Louis: C. V. Mosby Company, 1979.

7. Miller, D. K. and Allen, T. E. *Fitness: A Lifetime Commitment.* Minneapolis: Burgess Publishing Company, 1979.

8. Stc ᵔs, Roberta; Moore, A.; Moore, C.; and Williams, C. *Fitness: The New Wave.* Winston-Sale.n, North Carolina: Hunter Textbooks Inc., 1981.

Chapter 5
Warming Up and
Cooling Down

Whatever your training program, whether it be jogging, lifting weights, or playing a sport, remember each workout should consist of three essential phases: (1) **the warm-up,** (2) **the training session,** and (3) **the cool-down.** All three phases are very important for a program which will provide maximum results and optimum safety.

Beginning joggers wanting instant success are usually impatient and sometimes forego the warm-up and cool-down because of time. Unfortunately, such impatience impairs performance and invites pain and injury. A series of pre and post stretching activities can make the difference between enjoyment or pain and may determine whether you continue to participate in this healthful activity.

Repeated contraction of any muscle without opposing action tends to shorten the muscle during its resting state. The muscles gradually bunch up, harden, and lose their ability to change and move fluidly. These shortened muscles are likely to spasm, which is a common cause of post exercise pain and stiffness. Proper stretching exercises tend to lengthen the muscles and tendons, fill the muscles with blood and make them more supple. Needless to say, the more pliable the muscle or tendon is, the less likely strain or sprain will occur.

Another misconception of novices is their criterion for correct stretching. Unfortunately, some people believe that a bobbing or bouncing action using the body's momentum should be done until pain is achieved. Such an approach has proven unnecessary and even dangerous. In such ballistic stretching the stretch reflex mechanism is activated in an effort to protect the body from injury due to overstretching. This mechanism causes the muscles to contract and therefore resist the stretching motion. The pain that is felt as a result of improper stretching is the pain of contracting muscles.

Research has shown that soft tissues and muscles are affected best by a static stretch which does not activate the stretch reflex mechanism. In static stretching,

Static Stretching.

Ballistic stretching such as the four count toe touch can be hazardous.

Hold each stretch 15-30 seconds.

one holds the muscle to a greater than resting length in a stationary position for a period of time, usually 15-30 seconds. This slow, sustained method of stretching allows the muscles to relax and lengthen so increased flexibility can occur. Static stretching is less likely to injure tissues and cause muscle soreness than ballistic type stretching. In some cases, it has actually been shown to relieve muscle soreness.

If injuries are to be prevented, muscles must be stretched out regularly. How often is regular? For the jogger, stretching should be done at each workout. Of course, the more frequently one devotes time to improving flexibility, the more rapid the progress. So learn to enjoy stretching. Find ways to stretch here, there and everywhere, while watching television or while visiting a friend. However, unrealistic comparisons with the flexibility of others should not be made.

GUIDELINES FOR A FLEXIBILITY PROGRAM

1. Pre-activity stretching consisting of static poses will help your body to feel more like moving.

2. Before stretching, take a moment to make certain your posture is correct, and when possible, stretch in straight lines.

3. All stretching should be gradual and progressive. The best length of time for the stretch hold is 15-30 seconds.

4. Breathe normally. Do not hold your breath while stretching.

5. Flexibility development is specific. Exercises must be selected for each muscle group or joint in which flexibility is desired.

6. Ballistic stretching, bobbing or bouncing movements, should not be done. The stretch reflex mechanism may occur, thus causing soreness and possible damage to the soft muscle tissues, ligaments or tendons.

7. Stretching should be distributed rather than massed; thus, exercise should be performed several times a day and four or five days a week. More frequent stretching will result in greater flexibility.

8. Flexibility is specific to each individual. Stretch according to what you feel, not according to what others do.

9. Brief cardiorespiratory warm-ups such as walking fast, slow jogging or running in place are excellent. This warm-up is necessary to increase circulation and body heat for the tissues, ligaments, and joints, thus increasing flexibility of the muscle and skeletal systems.

10. Remember also to stretch after you workout so as to relax the contracted muscles and prevent soreness.

Jogging authorities agree that cooling down after a run is nearly as important as the warm-up. A progressive cool-down allows your breathing to return to normal, blood and other tissue fluids to be brought back into balance, and stiffness and soreness in tight muscles to be reduced.

If you suddenly stop your physical activity without a gradual cool-down period, blood tends to pool in the muscles that were active. This sometimes causes faintness since not enough blood is leaving those muscles for your brain.

A proper cool-down should begin by gradually decreasing your jogging pace. Having completed the run, continue to walk for 5-10 minutes, and swing your arms to increase circulation. Finally, repeat some of the same stretching exercises that you used for the warm-up.

STRETCHING EXERCISES

The exact type of stretching exercises for the jogger should be selected for those muscles which shorten as a result of the activity. For example, runners need to stretch the Achilles tendons, calves, quadriceps, groin, hamstrings and lower back. The following exercises are just a few of the innumerable stretches for these regions.

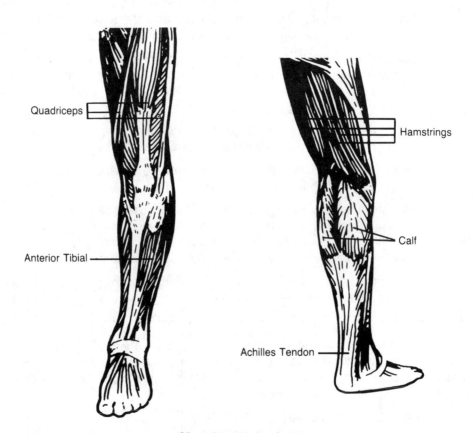

Muscles of the Leg

LIMBER UP Shoulder, pectoral, lateral abdominal stretches

— Stand erect with feet shoulder-width apart.

— Slowly stretch both arms as high as possible and hold.

— Slowly bend to one side as far as possible and hold.

— Slowly stretch to the other side and hold.

— Raise arms to shoulder level and slowly turn to your left, looking over shoulder and hold. Repeat in opposite direction.

— With arms over head, slowly bend the head back.

— Hold each position for 5 seconds.

PECTORAL STRETCH

— Stand facing the back
of a chair or other ob-
ject.

— Reach forward and
grasp the back of the
chair.

— Bend forward and
draw head and chest
downward by con-
tracting the abdomi-
nal muscles, keeping
the lower back flat
with little arch.

— Hold position for 15
seconds.

BACK EXTENSORS STRETCH

— Place your hands and knees on the floor.

— Slowly tuck your chin and round your back, lifting it as high as possible.

— Hold position for 15 seconds then raise your head and return to original
position and repeat.

CROSS LEG (HAMSTRING) STRETCH

— Stand straight with right leg crossed over left leg, feet together and parallel.

— Place right hand on left shoulder.

— Bend forward *slowly* and stretch.

— Keep knees straight.

— Hold position for 15 seconds.

— Repeat with left leg crossed over right leg.

HAMSTRING STRETCH

— Prop one leg on a chair, table, bench, or other object.

— With raised leg straight, hips even, bend forward from the hips until you feel the stretch in the back of your thigh.

— Hold for count of 15 seconds.

— Do the same with other leg supported.

QUADRICEPS STRETCH

— Balance yourself with left hand resting against wall.

— Flex right leg to the rear and grasp the ankle with your right hand.

— As you pull against your raised leg, lean forward at the waist until the stretch in the front of the leg is felt.

— Hold position for 15 seconds.

— Repeat for left leg.

GROIN STRETCH

— Sit on the floor with back straight.

— Place the soles of your feet together.

— Reach forward with your hands to grasp the feet.

— Pull your feet a comfortable distance in from your groin.

— Slowly bend forward from the hips until tension is felt in the thighs and groin.

— Hold the stretch for 15 seconds.

ACHILLES TENDON STRETCH

— Stand with feet flat and apart, slightly more than arms' length from the wall.

— With both hands flat on the wall, bend the elbows and lean forward until tension is felt in your calves.

— Keep the knees and body straight.

— Hold this position for 15 seconds.

— For more intensity, place a book under the balls of your feet.

CALF STRETCH

— Stand 3½ feet to 4 feet from a wall.

— Place your right foot one pace ahead of the left.

— Lean forward, supporting yourself against the wall with your hands, keeping heels flat.

— Slowly bend the knee of the left leg until maximum stretch is accomplished in the Achilles.

— Hold position for 15 seconds, then back off slowly.

— Repeat with right foot in the rear position.

KNEE-CHEST PULL

— Lie on your back with legs extended.

— Bring one knee to the chest, keeping extended leg straight and on the floor.

— Grab the knee with both hands and hold for 15 seconds.

— Return to starting position and repeat with opposite leg.

— This exercise may be done standing on one leg and bringing the other to the chest.

SUPPLEMENTARY EXERCISES FOR STRENGTH

When jogging, the muscles in the back of the leg become stronger than those in the front. With such a muscle imbalance, it becomes important to engage in exercises that strengthen the muscles in the front of the leg.

SHIN MUSCLE

— Sit on a table that will allow the legs to hang without touching floor.

— Place a light weight over the toes and flex the ankle.

— Repeat eight to fifteen times with each leg.

QUADRICEPS MUSCLES

— Sit on a table with legs hanging over edge.

— Straighten the leg against a resistance.

— Repeat eight to fifteen times with each leg.

ABDOMINAL MUSCLES

— Assume bent-knee sit-up position.

— Curl up to a sitting position, first the head, then the shoulders, and finally the back.

— Uncurl and return to starting position.

— Progressively increase the number of repetitions and/or degree of incline.

REFERENCES

1. Brody, Jane E. "Before – After Stretches May Save Jock Some Grief." Gainesville (Florida) *Sun*, December 18, 1981.

2. Couch, Jean. "Stretching Facts on the Achilles Tendon." *Runner's World,* May 1980, pp. 41-43.

3. Cundiff, D. and Brunteson, P. *Health Fitness Guide to a Lifestyle.* Dubuque, Iowa: Kendall/Hunt Publishing Company, 1979.

4. DeVries, Herbert A. "Electromyographic Observations of the Effects of Static Stretching Upon Muscular Distress." *Research Quarterly* 32:468-79, 1961.

5. Editors of *Runner's World. Exercises for Runners.* Mountain View, California: World Publications, Inc., 1980.

6. Editors of *Runner's World. Running After 40.* Mountian View, California: World Publications, Inc., 1980.

7. Hockey, R. *Physical Fitness: The Pathway to Healthful Living.* St. Louis: C. V. Mosby Company, 1979.

8. Larson, L. A., ed. *Encyclopedia of Sport Sciences and Medicine.* New York: The Macmillan Company, 1979.

9. Miller, D. K. and Allen, T. E. *Fitness: A Lifetime Commitment.* Minneapolis: Burgess Publishing Company, 1979.

10. Stokes, Roberta; Moore, A.; Moore, C.; and Williams, C. *Fitness: The New Wave.* Winston-Salem, North Carolina: Hunter Textbooks Inc., 1981.

Chapter 6
Developing Your Style

Often the first thing a person thinks about when considering whether to start a jogging program is "How will I look? Will I look like a runner?" It seems the less a person has engaged in physical activity the more likely he or she is to be concerned about technique. Such concerns are unnecessary since there is no single correct way to jog. So just do what comes naturally. Since no two people are built anatomically the same, each person will have his or her own distinctive natural style that is as different among joggers as fingerprints. The important thing is to follow basic mechanical principles which will prevent injuries and make your body more energy efficient.

DEVELOPING FORM

Body Position

The best jogging posture is an erect position, keeping the back comfortably straight and almost perpendicular to the ground. While the spine should be straight, it should not be locked in place. The goal is to center most of the body weight over the hips. To run upright or to "run tall" you should pull the shoulders back and tuck the pelvis in, so as to move it forward in relation to the rest of the body. This will help to straighten the spine and maintain the body in an upright position. **Do not look at your feet,** but keep the head level by looking as far ahead as possible. The face, neck, and shoulder muscles should be relaxed. In other words, the same straight posture that was taught in elementary school is also necessary for jogging. The only difference is that you are just a little more relaxed.

Keeping arms relaxed and using a natural stride insure good jogging form.

Arm Action

Since hands and arms influence body movement, these parts have an important function and should move rhythmically with the legs. As the pace is increased, the hands will rise higher at the beginning of each swing. Therefore, the arc of the arm swing will vary with your pace.

There is no universal pattern of arm carriage. Most authorities agree, however, that while jogging (a slow pace in which a conversation with a partner can be maintained) the elbows should be in a state of poised relaxation with arm movement held to a minimum. The arms should be in a position to fight off tension, neither rigid nor completely relaxed. The hand and elbow should be

Clenched fist with arms carried high drain energy.

Arms lose much of their balancing and driving function when allowed to come across the body.

Correct arm carriage is energy efficient.

approximately parallel to the ground, swinging no more than a foot and slightly in front of the body as the leg on the opposite side moves back.

The hands should be lightly cupped but not clenched. The tips of the fingers should be touching, with the thumb making a circle with the forefinger. Cupping the hands in this manner and keeping the arms relaxed will help ward off tension leading to unnecessary fatigue. It is also a good idea to loosely shake the shoulder and arms now and then to make sure they stay relaxed.

Stride and Foot Plant

The entire stride is divided into two phases, the contact phase or footplant and the swing phase. The movement is initiated with a push-off diagonally backward with the ball and toes of one foot. After the push-off is made, the leg swings forward as flexion is initiated at the hip joint, then the knee and the ankle lift the foot clear of the ground. As the foot again contacts the ground, the weight is transferred from the heel along the outer edge of the foot to the ball and to the toes as the next push-off is made.

The foot plant is one of the most important factors in the mechanics of jogging. One common error made by beginning joggers is running on the toes. Only sprinters, who run short distances, run on their toes. Joggers who run long distances on their toes frequently suffer a very painful leg condition called "shin splints."

All runners plant the feet the same way at a particular pace. The method in which the foot is planted changes only as speed increases or slows down. The foot plant continuum related to speed and distance is illustrated on the next page. With walking on one end of the continuum, there is a slower pace with the feet landing further back on the heel during each stride. On the other end of the continuum is sprinting, where the distance covered is shorter and much faster. The foot plant in this case is more toward the ball of the foot. While sprinters' heels almost never touch the ground, those running a mile or more should always run with a heel first contact.

Sprinting is for short distances.

The point of foot contact varies with speed and distance:

Heel first contact for
long runs and jogging

Metatarsal arch area
(looks as if contact is
made with entire foot)
becomes the contact
point for 800-1500
meter distances

Ball of foot is contact
point for 100-200 meter
sprints

Stride length, as with the foot plant, changes with pace. The slower the pace, the shorter the stride. As you speed up, the stride is lengthened. In running long distances the stride should be rather short, approximately four feet between footfalls. Of course, length of stride is an individual matter. You should have a

Overstriding results in a roller coaster action.

natural stride that feels comfortable to you. There are, however, two fundament-als you should remember to regulate stride length:

1. The foot should make contact with the ground after it has obtained the farthest point of advance.

2. The point of contact should be directly under the knee, not out in front of it. (1)

Both fundamentals will automatically occur if the knees are kept slightly bent at all times. When the foot is allowed to land ahead of the knee (overstriding), the leg is too straight and acts as a brake rather than an accelerator, resulting in wasted upward motion.

The point to remember is that both foot plant and stride length will shift with pace, much like a car shifting gears. The idea is to run in the right gear for the circumstance at hand.

Breathing

Breathing is, of course, the process of external respiration by which air is brought into the lungs so that the blood may absorb the oxygen and carry it to all parts of the body. Since it requires a lot of air to satisfy the body's need for oxygen while jogging, some attention should be given to the breathing action itself. Breathing should be as natural as possible by taking air in through both the mouth and nose. The action is not produced by the lungs, which remain passive, but by the contraction and relaxation of the diaphragm muscle. The diaphragm is the strong wall of muscle that separates the chest cavity from the abdominal cavity. When the diaphragm muscle contracts (moves downward), it creates a suction action in the chest drawing air in and expanding the lungs. When the muscle relaxes, the chest cavity decreases and the air is pushed out.

The most efficient method of breathing is abdominal. When inhaling, the diaphragm descends pushing the abdominal wall outward. Upon exhaling, the diaphragm rises and the abdomen flattens. One sign of improper breathing is a chest that overly expands when inhaling. Breathing abdominally may alleviate side aches known as stitches (sharp pains in the side area) and discomfort experienced by female joggers who wear a tight fitting bra. To practice this method of breathing, lie on the floor and place several books on the stomach. Make the books rise when inhaling and descend when exhaling.

One should also be conscious of breathing rhythmically. Breathing and stride generally are coordinated. So many strides per breath are taken, depending upon pace and fatigue. The value of breathing rhythmically may be more psychological than physical. When one is concentrating on a breathing pattern, it is easier to forget about being tired or bored and the miles will seem to fly.

Basic Mechanical Principles of Jogging

1. Erect body carriage or "running tall" provides maximum power and efficiency.

2. Arms have important balancing and driving functions. The arc of the arm swing varies with pace.

3. The progressive transference of weight from heel, to outside edge of foot, to toes, distributes the impact over a greater period of time.

4. Footfall and stride length relate to speed and distance, and must change as pace increases or decreases.

Common Jogging Faults

1. Landing on the ball of the foot or toes

2. Feet landing too far apart (overstriding)

3. Feet landing too close together (understriding)

4. Leaning too far forward

5. Excessive arm and hand movements

6. Hunched shoulders, elbows locked and hands clenched resulting in a tensed position

7. Overly expanding the chest to breathe

Key Points to Remember

1. Run erect and tall

2. Swing legs from hip with bent knees

3. Land on heel, allowing weight to roll along outside edge of foot to toes

4. Heel lands directly under knee

5. Point toes straight ahead

6. Keep arms and hands relaxed, swinging them forward easily

7. Breathe abdominally and in rhythm

Chapter 7
In Search of
the Perfect Shoe

Historians are not sure who made the first sneaker or what it looked like. What is known is that on May 19, 1832, Wait Webster of New York was granted a patent for a process of attaching India rubber soles to boots and shoes. In 1868 a company in Connecticut was licensed to make footware using the Goodyear vulcanization process. The shoe had a rubber sole, laces, and a canvas upper. However, it was not called a sneaker, tennis shoe, or running shoe, but a "croquet sandal." It was not until 1873 that the term "sneaker" was coined. (7)

Have you ever known anyone who did not own a pair of sneakers? It is estimated that 220 million pairs of sneakers are worn out each year in the United States alone. Over half of this number are imported from such countries as Taiwan, South Korea, and Japan. If you are counting, it adds up to billions of dollars in retail sales. (7)

By far the biggest reason for the sneaker explosion in the past decade has been the running shoe. Before the increased interest in jogging, there were only five or six quality brands from which one could choose a good running shoe; now there are over fifty. The reason for this manufacturing explosion is that running as a sport is growing (if you will excuse the expression) by leaps and bounds and as with any product, whether deodorants or microwave ovens, when something becomes popular, everyone wants some of the action.

Obviously, a simple sneaker is not designed to handle the constant pounding it would receive while jogging. One needs a masterfully constructed shoe, a veritable engineering truimph, which the shoe industry is happy to supply. Shoe manufacturers have responded to the growing market by developing a mystifying array of running shoes in innumerable designs, constructions, weights, materials, and colors. Some jogging shoes invariably look like they were put together by Dr. Frankenstein. Soles reach up from the floor, flared at the heel, with soles of studs, waffles, dimples, nubs, and other variations of the rubber cleat theme.

To say the least, this abundance of choice is confusing, not only for the beginning jogger, but for the more experienced one as well. Confusion is com-

pounded when viewing advertisements in running magazines that show diagrams of the inside of the shoe and its special features. If this is not enough to make a person timid about buying running shoes, one can visit a track and hear all the pros talking about absorption ratings, various wedges, and rear foot stabilizers.

Certainly there is a lot to learn about running shoes, but one should not have to earn an engineering degree to buy a pair. A beginner should be able to learn in fifteen minutes how to buy the right running shoe. A checklist is provided on page 65 to assist in finding the right pair for you.

Since shoes are the most important item of jogging equipment, everything else should take a back seat to what is covering the feet. One can wear old shorts and a baggy sweatshirt, but the feet must be well protected. Primitive man may very well have scampered barefoot over hills and valleys in pursuit of his dinner, but he was not running on asphalt or concrete.

A jogger's feet strike the ground approximately 1,600 times per mile. (7) At the rate of fourteen miles per week, this adds up to over one million foot falls a year. That is quite a pounding, and emphasizes why shoes are the first and most important investment for a jogger. The rule of thumb is: the less exercise one is accustomed to, the greater the need for a well-built pair of running shoes. Jogging is much harder on your body at the beginning stage of a program. Since many joggers are overweight, extra cushioning and support are needed and only quality running shoes can provide such support. Remember, proper shoes are an insurance policy toward preventing injuries, not only to the feet, but also to the legs, knees, hips, and lower back. This is true whether one is a beginning jogger

or a world class marathoner. In addition, quality running shoes can also enhance performance. The final reason for buying good shoes is psychological. There is more of a commitment to continue a newly initiated jogging program if a $30 to $50 investment has been made in a pair of running shoes. Needless to say, you will feel more like a runner if you are shod like one.

What kind of shoes should be purchased? Running shoes can be sorted into four categories: training shoes, racing shoes, sprint spikes, and distance spikes. For our purposes, we will discuss only the training shoes, some of which could be used for racing. There are three major differences between training and racing shoes. Training shoes are heavier, have higher heels, and thicker soles.

There is no such thing as the perfect shoe for everyone's needs. Each individual must experiment to determine which is best for her/himself. The process of buying a shoe should begin well before the actual purchase. You should first review the latest issue of *Runner's World* magazine that contains the annual ratings of various shoe brands and models. The magazine conducts laboratory tests on shoes to evaluate rearfoot control, impact protection, sole wear, flexibility, and traction. A choice of any shoe from the group obtaining the highest ranking (five stars) would more than meet the needs of the average jogger. Back issues should be available at any school or public library.

Examine your old shoes for worn spots, fabric creasing and lumps. Such areas indicate where your feet are trying to make adjustments. It may be a good idea to take them with you to the store for the salesperson to view. The soles of your old shoes provide many clues as to how you run and how your weight is transferred along your foot.

1. **Normal Wear Pattern:** The sole will show that the initial impact is on the outer side of the heel. The weight moves along the outer side of the foot and is transferred to an area between the first and second metatarsals. Runners with a faster pace will have a third wear spot on the tip of the shoe.

2. **Pronation:** When a jogger has fallen arches the foot turns downward toward the inner surface. Wear spots may be seen on the inner side of the sole. Such individuals are subject to pain in the back, leg, and arch.

3. **Supination:** The feet do not turn in properly and weight falls toward the outside edge of the sole. Knee problems may result from such a condition.

4. **Sesamoiditis:** An individual with bony feet may develop a wear spot behind the big toe. A bone bruise may develop where the first metatarsal sticks out.

5. **Depressed Metatarsal Arch:** Excessive wear behind the second and third toes is indicative of this condition. Development of corns and calluses in this region are results.

Once in the store, do not be overwhelmed by displays of different models or by the salesperson. In some cases, the salesperson will be operating on the premise that time is money and, therefore, will be anxious to put any pair of shoes on the customer's feet and send them on their way. Please take plenty of time, as it is your money and your feet. You should be prepared to find the best shoe that fits your running style, foot size, foot shape, body weight, and jogging surface. After trying on several different pairs for general comfort, do not hesitate to jog in place for a few minutes to determine comfort. The best time to fit yourself for a running shoe is in the late afternoon or evening, after tramping on your feet all day. That is when they are the largest. Another good idea is to wear the same kind of sock you will wear while jogging.

Today's shoe "sizes" have become a bit more scientific than when they were first created during the reign of King Edward II. At that time thirty-nine barleycorns in a row were classified as a size thirteen. (7) Shoe stores now use two very accurate devices for measuring shoe size: the Ritz Stick and the Brannock Metal Fitting Tray. Both feet should be measured, with shoes purchased for the larger one. A heel cushion or an innersole can be added to the shoe for the smaller foot.

Shoe size does not remain the same after adulthood. For example, if you gain weight, your feet may increase one shoe size. Since most running shoes are sized smaller than street shoes, be prepared to try on a size seven and a half if you normally wear a six. Sizes also vary from one manufacturer to another since they are made on different lasts.

Insist on having your foot measured.

Toe box should be adequate.

Length

When measuring for length, the end of the big toe should be at least ½" from the front tip of the shoe. Some experts even advise a ¾" gap. This space helps accommodate for foot expansion. Notice the heel counter; if a finger can be placed between it and your foot, the shoe does not fit. The heel should fit snugly. If your toes have to be closer or farther back from the front of the shoe than the above measurements to insure proper width, then the shoes are too narrow or too wide for your feet.

Width

Width is absolutely critical. Unfortunately, most manufacturers do not make shoes in specific widths. Most shoes on the market are made in the American "C" or "D" width for men and "B" width for women. New Balance is one company making a serious effort to help runners who do not have average feet. They offer widths from AA to EEE. Be sure to have the width measured at the same time as the length. The width is correct when the feet feel firmly enclosed, yet not too snug nor squeezed. When laces extend more than ½" side to side, the shoe is too narrow. Individuals with wide feet should investigate Puma (built on an E last). Those with narrow feet may want to try Adidas. If feet are a B width, use an insole to reduce the width of the shoe by one letter.

Shoe Sole

Most runners agree that the sole is the most important part of the shoe. Not only does it have to support the foot and protect against sharp objects that may be stepped on, it also has to cushion the foot against constant pounding. It is estimated that 80 percent of the body weight is supported by four or five square inches of heel surface, as the foot strikes the ground. (7) For a 150-pound runner, the load would be 24 pounds per square inch at rest, and somewhat higher for impact forces on landing. The rest of the foot serves as either balance, or on take-off, as a lever for the application of power in the pushoff. This is a lot of weight and a lot of shock and is the cause of most running injuries.

Composition of sole material is extremely important. The best running shoes have two or three layers of rubberized material that vary in thickness from toe to heel. A tough outer layer (the part that actually strikes the ground) made of high-density rubber will do a sufficient job of neutralizing shock and, of course, will last longer. Stay away from polyurethane soles, since they are too hard and have little shock absorbency. This outer layer should be wider than the others since a flared heel design distributes the impact over a larger area. Therefore, more shock-absorbing material is utilized during each landing.

Now look for a second layer, called the heel wedge, running from the heel to the ball of the foot. This slight elevation of the heel takes some of the strain off the Achilles tendons and also provides increased shock protection. The ideal heel lift between the heel and the toes of the shoe is debatable, but most experts agree that at least one-half inch of heel lift is necessary.

A third layer (midsole) of rubberized materials, runs from heel to toe. This layer is very important, since it is the only cushion provided for the mid-foot. Some shoe manufacturers color the different shoe sole layers. This technique is useful when checking the soles and heels to determine wear.

The sole must also provide good traction. The type of sole needed is determined by the type of surface upon which you jog. There are many variations in sole patterns but, in general, urban joggers who must jog on hard surfaces such as asphalt and cement need more shock absorption and less tread. A ripple-type sole works best under these conditions. Bottoms with rubber studs, nobs, or nipples are best on slick surfaces such as mud or grass. However, some gripper soles tend to wear quickly when used extensively on cement.

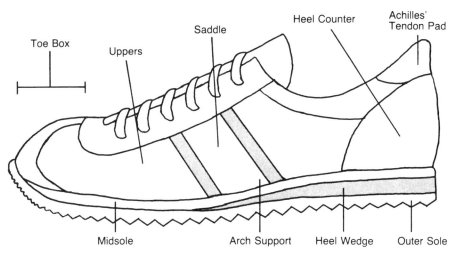

Construction of Running Shoe

A waffle type tread emphasizes cushioning and traction over durability.

Wear

Most running shoes wear along the rear outside edge of the sole because the foot scuffs forward into its initial contact position on the ground. If the foot landed like a helicopter, and immediately came in contact with the ground where contact forces are the largest, there would be almost no wear at all.

Obviously, the jogger must be concerned with potential wear characteristics of a shoe, since it is an important economic factor. The faster a shoe wears, the sooner a replacement will be needed. If wear is ignored, injuries to the knee and muscles can result, since the foot's interaction with the ground will be changed by the uneven outer sole.

Some companies have begun to construct shoes with the outer sole made of two components. Regions of high wear are cut away and a section of good abrasive rubber applied. To use this material for the entire sole would make the shoe too heavy and expensive. Some manufacturers have attempted to confuse the buyer by applying a light coat of paint over the rear outside corner to make it appear that a different type of rubber was used for this area. A built-up tread pattern on the rear outside border is almost a universal feature in all shoes whether they offer more abrasive rubber in the contact area or not.

Flexibility

Shoes should be flexible enough to conform with foot movement. With each running stride, the foot rolls forward at a 35-degree angle pushing off from the toes. Most doctors believe that if running shoes do not bend under the ball of the foot, excessive stress will be placed on the legs causing shin and Achilles tendon injuries. When selecting your shoe, flex the front one-third of the shoe, since this will be where the front one-third of the foot will be located. This bending of the sole is a test for flexibility. If the shoe bends too easily, this may be an indication that it lacks the qualities necessary for cushioning.

Flexibility will increase as shoes are broken in. Bend the shoes back and forth several times before jogging. Another way to increase the flexibility of shoes is to bend them at the ball of the foot and tape them in this position overnight.

Shoe Uppers

Most uppers for running shoes are made of nylon, suede, leather, or combinations. Many of today's running shoes have nylon or synthetic uppers because of their light weight, quick drying characteristics, and good ventilation. Because the inside of a running shoe is usually damp, dark, and warm, it offers a perfect environment for fungal and bacterial growth. Therefore, the control of temperature and humidity inside a running shoe becomes very important.

On the other hand, leather, while not providing the quality of good ventilation, does wear longer than nylon and offers better support. Another disadvantage of leather shoes is their susceptibility to water. When they become wet, they can stay soggy for days and when they do dry, they are often stiff and brittle, causing blisters.

With nylon uppers, you need not worry about moisture. Simply stuff them with newspaper and dry them at room temperature. Do not use the oven, hair dryer or strong sunlight for drying, as this may cause the soles to separate from the uppers. Leather uppers should be treated with castor oil or some other preservative to extend their life. Under no circumstances should any type of running shoe be thrown into the washing machine.

Inside the Shoe

To check the inside of a running shoe, rub your finger along the inside to see if there are any rough seams or edges that may cause blisters. All insole material should be soft and smooth. An arch support is absolutely essential and should either be built in or glued inside the shoe. Be certain the toe box has enough room. The height of the toe box should be sufficient to prevent unnecessary rubbing on the top of the toes, since this is the chief cause of toe blood blisters.

Heel Counters

Another desirable feature in a shoe is the property of rearfoot control. This is the extent to which the shoe supports the foot at ground contact, with respect to pronation or side-to-side foot roll. To help keep the foot firmly on the shoe platform, a shoe must have a cup made of reinforced leather located between the layers of the upper heel area. Shoes with a firmly padded heel counter "lock" the heel in place and prevent lateral movement, thus preventing painful blisters and possible stress that could cause damage to the foot, ankle, or leg. Such inno-vations by manufacturers as separate lacing for the rearfoot and removable mid-sole plugs are additional attempts to improve rearfoot control.

Achilles Tendon Pad

The final feature of a good upper is the protection offered at the top of the heel for the insertion of the Achilles tendon. The most critical point is where the tendon inserts into the groove of the heelbone. With each stride, there may be as much as one to two inches of movement involved. During a long run the tendon can become very tender at this point causing inflammation and formation of calcium deposits.

Shoe Weight

Marathoners usually select the lightest shoe they can find, but when buying a training shoe look more for support and cushioning, with weight not being that important. If speed is desired then runners usually choose to sacrifice support for lightness. Shoes weighing between ten and twelve ounces (283-340 grams) provide the right protection and support for training purposes. Generally, racing shoes are 25 percent lighter than training shoes, with the lightest ones being around 155 grams.

In a study conducted at Valparaiso University in Indiana, it was found that added shoe weight slightly increased heart rate and was only important at high speed. The study further concluded that at low stress paces, the body apparently adapts easily to the slight extra load. (2)

Feet are a jogger's natural resource and must be well cared for. Since a significant number of foot injuries occur because of the failure to wear proper shoes, selection of good running shoes is the most important and the only necessary investment really needed to become actively involved in a jogging program. The following checklist could be taken to your shoe store to assist in finding a pair of running shoes to fit individual needs.

Some shoes feature a removable innersole.

GUIDELINES FOR BUYING SHOES

When selecting running shoes, look for these features:

1. Multi-layer sole — a durable outer layer and an inner layer to absorb shock

2. Flexibility under the forefoot

3. Elevated heel — about one-half inch higher than the toes, tends to take strain off Achilles tendons

4. Wide heel bottom (flared heel) — distributes impact over a wider area and helps stabilize the foot

5. Heel counter — heel area stabilized by a rigid counter or cup

6. Padding for the Achilles tendon and ankle area

7. Upper made of soft, nonirritating material that has good ventilation and drying qualities

8. Adequate built-in arch support

9. Toe box height — adequate space for toes to spread out

10. Correct size — should be wide enough and long enough

REFERENCES

1. Cooper, Kenneth A. *The Aerobics Way.* New York: M. Evans and Company, Inc., 1977.

2. Editors of *Runners World. The Complete Runner.* Mountain View, California: World Publications, 1974.

3. Fisher, A. Garth and Allsen, Philip E. *Jogging.* Dubuque: Wm. C. Brown, 1980.

4. Geline, Rober J. *The Practical Runner.* New York: Collier Books, 1978.

5. Henderson, Joe. *Jog, Run, Race.* Mountain View, California: World Publications, 1977.

6. "Sixth Annual *Runner's World* Special Shoe Survey." *Runner's World,* October 1981, pp. 36-65.

7. Walker, Samuel A. *Sneakers.* New York: Workman Publishing Company, 1978.

8. Weisenfeld, Murray F. and Burr, Barbara. *The Runner's Repair Manual.* New York: St. Martin's Press, 1980.

9. Zimmermann, Caroline A. *The Super Sneaker Book.* Garden City, New York: Doubleday & Company, Inc., 1978.

Chapter 8
Dressing
for the Elements

Since jogging is not a seasonal sport, but one that is performed year round, be prepared to venture out into a variety of weather conditions. After all, for a jogging program to have lasting value, you cannot limit your running to fair weather. In fact, the warm, sunny days in which most sedentary people choose to venture outdoors are not as nice for the jogger as they may appear. Most joggers prefer overcast and cool days rather than sunshine.

Varying weather conditions dictate appropriate dress. You should dress one way for hot weather, another for cold, and differently when the humidity is extremely high or when it is raining or windy. Ideal jogging conditions, between 40° and 80° Fahrenheit (F), require only a basic uniform such as T-shirt, shorts, appropriate undergarments, socks and shoes.

As indicated in Chapter 7, shoes are the most important item of a jogger's wardrobe. Other clothing is unimportant except for comfort and suitability to weather conditions. In most cases, a simple jogging wardrobe can be obtained from your closet. There is no need to run up a clothing bill by outfitting yourself as if you are headed for the ski slopes. Your money can best be spent on a good pair of running shoes.

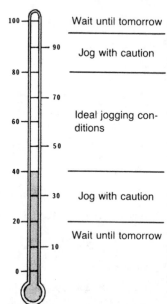

For temperature between 80-95°F and 20-40°F you should jog with caution. Once temperature goes above 95° or below 20°F, it's best to wait until another day or do some aerobic activity indoors.

Shirts

One of the best tops to train in is the standard T-shirt. Such shirts are predominantly cotton, which provides excellent absorbency and allows the body to breathe. In addition, they are comfortable, inexpensive, durable and easy to wash. Nylon tops are not absorbent and trap too much water, making cooling difficult. As for colors, common sense tells us to wear a white shirt in hot weather to reflect the sun and that dark colored shirts should never be worn at dusk or night.

Shorts

Our principle concern here is that you choose shorts that aren't too tight around the thighs or crotch and therefore rub and chafe the body. It is estimated that 80 percent of all running shorts are made of nylon. Nylon tricot is lightweight, dries quickly, and is nonabrasive.

While 50 percent polyester/50 percent cotton shorts have good absorbency, they are bulky, heavy and cause chafing. The material does retain heat well, but too much retention may saturate the shorts with perspiration, causing chafing.

In cold weather wear a nylon tricot short with a cotton brief to retain heat. In warm climate it may be helpful to wear similar shorts with a mesh brief. The mesh has excellent breathing characteristics and is helpful to those suffering from irritation or chafing.

One helpful hint to reduce the chafing problem and to reduce irritation is to smear petroleum jelly on your legs where the shorts contact your skin.

Warm-up Suits

For the same reasons you avoid nylon shirts, you should avoid nylon warm-up suits. They do not allow body heat to escape. Suits made of cotton, partial cotton mix or knit polyester material are more suitable. Try to purchase a warm-up suit that has zippers in the jacket and legs, since such features allow you to adjust your clothing to regulate body heat. Stay away from pants with flared bottoms. Such pants are nice for tennis players or if you are fashion conscious, but for joggers they let in air and just get in the way.

Socks

There are two primary reasons for wearing socks. Both reasons are economic and health related. Most joggers would agree that it is easier to wash socks than shoes. Wearing running shoes without clean socks means more frequent washing and therefore a shortened life span.

Socks also prevent direct friction of the skin against the shoe which causes blisters. Most runners prefer socks made of cotton, orlon or wool mixed with some nylon. It's not only good hygiene to always wear clean socks, but it's a fact that dirty socks are harder on the feet. In general, two pairs of socks are better than one. The combination of a thin pair of cotton socks against the foot and a thicker pair over them gives the most comfort and anti-blister protection. Regardless of the number of socks worn, be sure that your socks fit and there are no wrinkles or folds in them before putting on your shoes.

Supporting Undergarments

For men, a supporting undergarment means an athletic supporter; for women, a bra. The primary consideration in either case is comfort, support and prevention of chafing. In general, men's shorts having built-in linings provide sufficient support for the genitals. The same results may be obtained by wearing a pair of cotton or nylon briefs under athletic shorts. Jock straps are not ruled out, but they do sometimes bind and cause chafing.

Most women feel uncomfortable if their breasts are not firmly supported while jogging. Some report suffering from a condition known as jogger's nipple. The nipple becomes raw and bleeds as a result of excessive chafing against the bra or, if no bra is worn, against the shirt. To protect the breasts, a well fitting bra providing good upward support should be worn. A number of excellent sports bras are now on the market. It would be advisable to try on several different styles of sports bras and move around, mimicking the motions the breasts would undergo while jogging, then select the one best meeting your needs.

Rubberized Clothing

Rubberized clothing is a gimmick to "lose weight" and should be avoided, especially in hot, humid weather. The extra heat you generate while exercising is trapped inside the suit, thus raising the temperature and causing increased sweating. The net result is temporary water loss which is gained back within hours. What is more critical is the potential danger such attire can cause to your body when worn in hot, humid weather. Rubberized suits worn in cool weather can also be hazardous since chilling can result due to lack of sweat evaporation.

TEMPERATURE PROBLEMS

To determine the safety of jogging in hot and cold weather, you must know the temperature, wind velocity, and relative humidity. Usually this information can be obtained through radio and television broadcasts, over special weather radio channels, or by the telephone company's weather report number.

With such weather data, you may then refer to the charts provided (Tables 6 and 7) to find out if it is safe to jog. For temperature between 80° and 95°F, and 20° and 40° F, you should jog with caution. Once the temperature rises above 95° or drops below 20° it's best to wait until another day or do an indoor aerobic activity such as rope skipping, or running in place. Most people recognize the dangers associated with cold weather, but fail to realize that hot days can be even more serious for the jogger.

Hot Weather Dangers

Jogging when the temperature is ideal will reduce your chances of having to worry about the three hot weather dangers: heat cramps, heat exhaustion, and heat stroke. Heat is the most dangerous of the natural enemies the jogger must face. While jogging, the body acts as a heat-producing machine converting glycogen and fats into mechanical energy to activate the muscles. Studies have shown body temperature regularly rises in excess of 105° after runs of six miles or more. If the body's regulatory mechanisms malfunction and are unable to dissipate all the heat, major organs of the body (heart, brain, kidney, and liver) can be damaged.

Primary methods used by the body to counterbalance overheating (hypothermia) involve convection, radiation, and evaporation of sweat. When you first begin to exercise, blood flow is redirected toward the working muscles, causing a heat buildup. The flow of blood then distributes the heat throughout the body, particularly to the skin. Heat is thus conducted to the surface as well as directly transferred from muscles lying close to the skin. Circulating air currents convect the heat away.

Once the outside temperature rises above skin temperature (90°), heat loss through convection and radiation comes to an end. In fact, they may reverse their direction and add heat. At this stage, the only means the body has to counteract overheating is through evaporation of sweat.

Perspiration is released from the sweat glands beneath the skin surface. Body heat causes sweat to evaporate, thereby lowering the skin temperature. Every jogger needs to understand, however, that sweating in itself does not dissipate heat. Sweat that simply "rolls off" may be ineffective due to high humidity or restrictive clothing. **No heat can be lost unless there is evaporation.** In a hot, humid environment where the air is full of moisture, evaporative cooling is impaired because there is no place for the liquid sweat to go. This is why humid days seem hotter than dry ones, even though the temperature may be identical.

Joggers who exercise in the heat can also become dehydrated since much fluid is lost due to evaporation. It is highly important to avoid dehydration by replacing lost fluids.

TABLE 6
TEMPERATURE-HUMIDITY INDEX

Temperature (°F)

Humidity	70	75	80	85	90	95	100	105	110
10%	64	67	69	72	74	77	79	82	84
20%	65	67	70	73	76	79	82	84	87
30%	65	68	72	75	77	81	84	87	90
40%	66	69	73	76	79	83	86	90	93
50%	67	70	74	78	81	85	89	92	96
60%	67	71	75	79	83	87	91	95	
70%	68	72	76	80	85	89	93		
80%	69	73	78	82	87	91	95		
90%	69	74	79	84	88	93			
100%	70	75	80	85	90	95			

SAFE   CAUTION   DANGER

If you choose to jog during the caution zone, be sure to consume adequate fluids. It is considered unsafe to jog when the temperature – humidity index is in the danger zone.

Hot Weather Clothing

Since clothing can interfere with evaporation of sweat, it should be minimized when jogging at temperatures between 40° and 80°F (4° and 27°C). The basic jogger's outfit — T-shirt, shorts, undergarments, socks, and shoes supplemented with a hat on sunny days — is all that is necessary. If such clothing does not keep you cool consider changing your pace (hot weather causes your heart to beat faster) or your routine. Wait until the temperature cools off in the evening or run early in the morning. If the humidity is above 80 percent, postpone your jog to another day. Some days are just too hot and humid for your body to cool itself adequately. In addition to air temperature, be conscious of road heat if you jog on hard surface roads. Road heat can also quickly push temperatures past the caution zone.

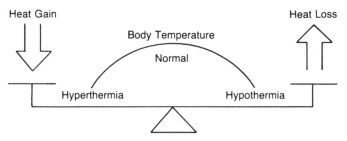

*When the body is unable to maintain equilibrium between heat loss and heat gain, hypothermia or heat exhaustion may result.

Cold Weather Problems

While getting rid of body heat is a summer problem, you must be concerned about losing too much body heat in the winter. This condition is know as hypothermia and can be caused by cold weather conditions and wet clothes.

FIVE WAYS TO LOSE BODY HEAT

Radiation is the leading cause of heat loss. An unprotected head may lose up to 50 percent of the body's total heat production at 40°F.

Conduction Contact with anything cooler than the skin temperature contributes to heat loss. Avoid exercises that require you to sit or lie on the ground during cold weather.

Convection The primary function of clothing is to retain a layer of radiated warm air close to the body. Cooler air passing the body tends to remove this warm air. The faster the wind (exchange of air), the greater the body heat loss.

Evaporation of sweat from the skin also contributes to heat loss. Wet clothing can extract heat from your body *240 times* faster than dry clothing. Wear wool when possible.

Respiration Inhaling cool air and exhaling warm air accounts for significant heat loss. To decrease loss of body heat due to respiration, preheat air by breathing through a scarf or ski mask.

(From U.S. National Park Service, Fatigue Exhaustion, Washington, D.C.: Government Printing Office)

Another cause is the impact that wind velocity has on temperature. The results can be measured and is called the wind chill factor. For each mile per hour of headwind, the air feels about one degree colder. If, for example, the thermometer indicated 40°F, a 20 m.p.h. wind can chill the air to 20°F as noted in Table 7. While

TABLE 7
WIND-CHILL EQUIVALENT TEMPERATURE TABLE

Temperature (°F)

Calm	40	35	30	25	20	15	10	5	0	−5	−10	−15	−20

Equivalent Chill Temperature

Total Air Speed (M.P.H.)	40	35	30	25	20	15	10	5	0	−5	−10	−15	−20
5	35	30	25	20	15	10	5	0	−5	−10	−15	−20	−25
10	30	20	15	10	5	0	−10	−15	−20	−25	−35	−40	−45
15	25	15	10	0	−5	−10	−20	−25	−30	−40	−45	−50	−60
20	20	10	5	0	−10	−15	−25	−30	−35	−45	−50	−60	−65
25	15	10	0	−5	−15	−20	−30	−35	−45	−50	−60	−65	−75
30	10	5	0	−10	−20	−25	−30	−40	−50	−55	−65	−70	−80
35	10	5	−5	−10	−20	−25	−35	−40	−50	−60	−65	−75	−80
40	10	0	−5	−15	−20	−30	−35	−45	−55	−60	−70	−75	−85

CAUTION   DANGER   EXTREME DANGER

To determine the risk of jogging during cold weather, find the temperature at the top of the chart. Next add your speed to that of the wind and locate the total air speed to the left of the chart.

such weather may cause chapped lips and chilled faces, it is doubtful your lungs will freeze. This mythical ailment is widely feared by joggers but never experienced by them. Unless you have particular breathing problems, you should not have to worry about the cold if you jog within the area marked safe on the wind chill factor chart.

It should be noted, however, that jogging during the "caution" zone, especially with damp skin from perspiration or precipitation, can cause frostbite to exposed flesh.

Cold Weather Clothing

The only fashion principle applicable to cold weather jogging is to adapt the "layered look." Layers of loose fitting clothes, rather than heavier and tight ones, will not only allow you to move more freely and trap heat better, but also to peel away clothing as your body temperature increases.

Depending on how cold it is and your personal choice, it may be necessary to wear up to four layers.

First layer: Undergarments that are absorbent and nonirritating; wool socks.

Second layer: This layer provides insulation for the skin. You may choose long underwear or turtleneck shirt. The latter helps to retain heat usually lost around the neck.

Third layer: Long pants and a sweater, or warm-up suit go next. The old fleece-lined hooded sweat shirt that ties around the neck is ideal for this layer.

Fourth layer: This last layer is necessary only in extremely cold or windy weather and is made up of a light-weight wind breaker. If you are still cold, wear more layers, not heavier ones.

If the temperature falls below 40°F/4°C, it is a good idea to wear gloves and a hat, since considerable body heat can be lost at these points and there is the added possibility of frostbite. A ski mask may become necessary when encountering wind accompanied by low temperatures.

When planning your winter workout give consideration to the direction of the wind. It is best to go into the wind the first half of your run and jog with it on the way back. Jogging into the wind will provide some resistance, causing body heat to build. On the return trip, jogging with the wind will prevent you from having to face the wind in wet clothing.

As for materials, cotton is highly absorbent and serves as a good wick for perspiration to prevent chilling. Wool is also very absorbent and has the best insulation properties; therefore, it holds body heat much better than cotton.

REFERENCES

1. DeVries, Herbert A. *Physiology of Exercise.* Dubuque, Iowa: Wm. C. Brown, 1976.

2. Editors of *Runner's World. The Complete Runner.* Mountain View, California: World Publications, 1974.

3. Geline, Robert J. *The Practical Runner.* New York: Macmillan Publishing Co., Inc., 1978.

4. Gilmore, C. P. *Exercising for Fitness.* Alexandria, Virginia: Time-Life Books, 1981.

5. Haycock, Christine E. "Breast Problems – Jogging and Other Sports." *Nautilus Magazine,* August/September 1981, pp. 50-52.

6. Henderson, Joe. *Jog, Run, Race.* Mountain View, California: World Publications, 1977.

7. Hockey, R. *Physical Fitness: The Pathway to Healthful Living.* St. Louis: C. V. Mosby Company, 1973.

8. Miller, D. K. and Allen, T. E. *Fitness: A Lifetime Commitment.* Minneapolis: Burgess Publishing Company, 1979.

9. Pistilli, Jayanne. "Today's Running Clothes." *Runner's World,* July, 1980, pp. 70-71.

10. Ullyot, Joan. *Women's Running.* Mountain View, California: World Publications, 1976.

Chapter 9
Where to Jog — Jogging Routes and Surfaces

As a beginning jogger you are probably asking yourself, "Where is the best place to jog?" Technically, any place you can safely walk will do for jogging, but some places are better than others. Ideally, the best jogging environment should meet the following criteria:

1. **Convenience:** Close enough that you may start and finish near your home. Why waste time driving to a training site, not to mention the trouble?

2. **Smooth dirt or grass surface:** Such surfaces are easier on the legs than asphalt or concrete. Rough ground can also damage the ankles and knees.

3. **Inclines:** If you are an advanced runner you may seek out hills; otherwise be content on completing your distance on flat terrain.

4. **Free of auto traffic:** This will cut down on risk, air pollution, and self-consciousness.

5. **Free of animals, reptiles, and insects:** Jogging with a dog in hot pursuit is not the most enjoyable way to increase intensity.

6. **Pleasant surroundings:** A natural environment provides many pleasant things to look at and listen to. Such an environment will make the miles fly by, as well as provide shade and protection from wind.

Many nature lovers argue that the best things in life are free. Jogging enthusiasts draw the same conclusion when it comes to physical activity. They are quick to point out that one of the great advantages of jogging is that it can be done almost anywhere. There is no need for a pool, tennis court, Universal Gym or even a bicycle. While adequate jogging environments are more easily found than expensive facilities, individuals in an urban setting may find it difficult to find the "ideal" jogging route.

Obviously, the ideal jogging surface would be on dirt or grass with no incline and no holes. There is less possibility of injury while jogging on such a surface than what realistically is found by urban joggers.

74

COURSE SURFACES

The degree of impact upon landing and the amount of force necessary in your push-off is influenced by the surface you jog on. While a soft surface, such as sand, absorbs most of the 80 pounds per square inch exerted on your foot, it requires more effort during the push-off, since you must push back the soft surface. The reverse is true on a hard surface, such as concrete or asphalt.

Jogging on sand causes additional pull on the Achilles tendon when the heels sink into the surface. Individuals with shin splints, calf or Achilles problems and beginning joggers should jog under ideal conditions until their muscles and tendons are flexible enough for the pulling that jogging on sand will cause. If you must jog on the beach, run on the damp, firm portion that is near the water and avoid the soft, deep sand higher up on the beach.

The most available smooth surface without obstructions are roads, and since they are so accessible, this is where most people do their jogging. These joggers often encounter minor aches and pains from the constant pounding of jogging on asphalt or concrete; since these surfaces are not resilient the jogger must absorb the impact exerted. If you must jog on these hard surfaces, be sure your shoes have good cushioning.

You may want to add extra sponge lining to reduce the impact shock. Also, try to add some variation in your routes — don't jog the same way over the same course every day.

Dirt and grass surfaces without roots, holes and rocks are very good surfaces to jog on. These surfaces, along with oval tracks, are the most resilient surfaces and should be sought out by the beginning jogger. While the quarter-mile track is good for knowing exactly how far you are jogging, it can be very boring. The repetition of jogging around the same oval for miles might deter you from participation in the activity that could prolong your life.

Special Surfaces

Jogging through unplowed snow is much like jogging in sand. Impact is very light, but the amount of force necessary in the push-off is great. However, there are more safety hazards caused by jogging in snow than in sand. For example, the snow may be hiding a hole in the ground or some object which could cause you to twist an ankle or to trip.

When encountering slippery surfaces, such as ice or plowed snow, you will need to reduce the force exerted and to shorten the stride. This will provide a larger base for support and keep the center of gravity directly over the feet when the heel strikes the ground.

Inclines

Unless your jogging is confined to an oval track, you will probably encounter hills. During the initial phase of your program you may wish to map a route to avoid them. If you are having trouble with bruises on the ball of the foot, Achilles tendonitis, or shin splints, you may want to limit routes that include hills. Otherwise, hills can be a real plus, since jogging on hills puts more muscles into play, thereby requiring more energy. It has been estimated that jogging uphill at a 6 percent incline requires 35 percent more energy expenditure than jogging on flat terrain. Such stress on the body has made hill running and stadium step running a part of athletic coaches' training programs for years.

The basic element to remember when jogging uphill is to lean forward so the center of gravity is over the base of support. The more the incline, the more forward you must land on the foot, allowing for less heel impact. In jogging downhill you have gravity on your side. To regulate speed in your descent, lean backward to slow down and forward to increase speed.

COURSE ENVIRONMENT

For a number of reasons the jogger should choose a variety of environments. As with jogging on an oval track, one soon grows tired of jogging a single path. Variety in scenery can do much toward maintaining a healthy attitude toward jogging. Another factor is that some of the best routes (scenery wise) are often impassable in snowy or rainy weather, thus making alternate routes essential.

For the purposes of analyzing advantages and disadvantages of various jogging environments, the following divisions are offered:

Track

A 440 track provides a convenient standard for the jogger who wants to record precisely the distance covered and the time involved.

Advantages:

1. Surface provides good impact absorption
2. Convenient for determining distance and time
3. Provides contact with other joggers
4. Track atmosphere motivates many people to jog
5. Drinking fountains, showers, and lockers are usually available
6. Provides safe jogging environment

Disadvantages:

1. Boredom for those that bore easily, who may find they tire faster mentally

2. Inconvenient: Must travel to track and back, crowding, limited hours, and possible fees

3. Beginning joggers may become self-conscious when surrounded by "professionals"

Open Country

Many joggers are fortunate to have access to environments that are scenic, peaceful, and open. Jogging courses laid out over such an area could be compared to a cross-country course. The anticipation of viewing something different each day along the same route motivates many joggers to seek out such an environment.

Advantages:

1. Surface provides good impact absorption

2. Mentally relaxing

Disadvantages:

1. Possibility of injury due to uneven surface, rocks, and limbs

2. Encounters with reptiles and insects

3. Inconvenient for some urban dwellers

4. High crime areas during early morning and late evening hours, threat to personal safety

Roads and Sidewalks

Most joggers in today's society only have to open their door to reach a concrete surface that leads to a sidewalk or asphalt road. Such convenience entices joggers to run on these hard surfaces. If you must jog on asphalt or concrete, choose asphalt, since it is more resilient than concrete.

Advantages:

1. Convenience in this automotive age; few areas are without roadways

2. Smooth surface and few obstructions

Disadvantages:

1. Hard surface could result in minor injuries
2. Fatalities have resulted when joggers challenged cars for the right of way

Parcours

A parcour is an established route of considerable distance, frequently through wooded and irregular terrain. Exercise stations are alternated with periods of running as the course is traversed. Signs displaying drawings and descriptive information are posted at each exercise station.

Advantages:

1. Resilient surface
2. Scenic environment
3. Contact with other physical fitness enthusiasts
4. Develops all fitness components
5. Specific directions and goals posted

Disadvantages:

1. Accessibility
2. Possible threat to personal safety

Course Layout

While the course environment takes all elements into consideration, course layout deals specifically with the course route the jogger has chosen. You may apply any of the course layouts to the preceding environments.

Course layouts may be categorized in the following manner, each having its strong points and limitations.

Point to Point: Such a route gives the runner a feeling of accomplishment, since he or she starts at one point and finishes at another. While it is pleasant to run because there is no repetition, there is a problem of getting back to the original point.

Start  Finish

Laps: Repeating the same circular or oval track is ideal for monitoring intensity and duration of a run; however, if you bore easily this is not the layout you should choose.

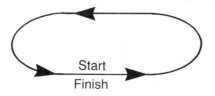

Out and Back: Here the jogger travels to a turn around point and then repeats the route back to the original starting point. Such a route is commonly used by beginners, since it enables them to meet or progressively increase their distance. One drawback for some joggers is that the course is repeated on the return trip.

Loop: Considering all factors, the loop route is probably the best all-around course layout. The same ground is never covered twice and a lot of territory can be covered. The main advantage is that the circuit begins and finishes at the same place.

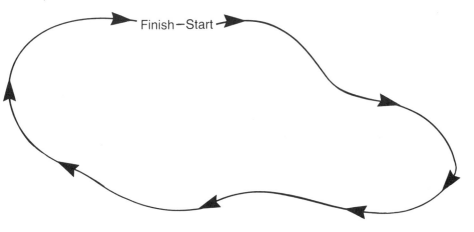

Following are five specific steps you will need to take in order to design a jogging course:

1. Decide on your course route.
2. Draw the course.
3. Measure the distance.
4. Consider danger points.
5. Draw the distance markers and other points you feel are important (wet places, loose rocks, etc.).

MEASURING COURSE

Knowing the distance of your jogging course is very important, since it enables you to apply the training principles discussed in Chapter 4. Without knowing the distance jogged, you have no objective measurement as to what degree the overload principle is being applied. Incorrect progression may retard your jogging program.

The most convenient way of checking the distance of a course is with a car odometer. One disadvantage to this method is that car measurements usually produce short courses. Another limiting factor is that some jogging courses may cover areas which cannot be traveled by car. A more precise measurement can be obtained with a bicycle counter. After calibrating it over a measured course, such as a 440 track, you should be able to determine the distance of your course within a yard per mile.

Another method is to simply walk off the necessary distance. This method is accomplished by measuring the length of your step in feet and inches and then calculating how many paces are necessary to equal 440 yards, 880 yards, a mile, or longer.

SAFETY CONSIDERATIONS FOR JOGGERS

Safety on the Road:

1. Avoid jogging during peak traffic periods.

2. Jog facing traffic.

3. Do not challenge autos; move to right of way when a car approaches.

4. Wear clothing drivers can see.

5. Do not run at night; if it is a must, wear a reflective vest or tape.

6. Obey all traffic signals and signs.

7. When crossing the road or an intersection, be alert and cross at a 90 degree angle.

A no-no.

8. Be on the lookout for protruding objects from passing cars or trucks.

Weather-related Conditions

1. On foggy days, wait until the fog lifts before jogging.

2. Avoid jogging when the pollution index is high.

3. Refrain from jogging on slippery surfaces such as snow and ice.

4. Dress appropriately for weather conditions (see Chapter 8).

Animal, Reptile, Insects, and Poisonous Plants

1. If you encounter unfriendly dogs, you have three alternatives: either make friends with them, speak to their owners about local leash laws, or find a new jogging course.

2. Watch out for snakes if your route takes you through wet, grassy, or rocky areas.

3. Be alert for nests of insects such as wasps or yellow jackets.

4. Be able to recognize and avoid poison oak, poison ivy, and poison sumac.

Personal Safety

1. Female joggers should run with a partner.

2. Carry some form of identification and your phone number in case of emergency.

3. Check out approaching joggers. If they appear suspicious, cross the street.

4. Keep an eye out for unusual sounds or movement in dark or bushy areas.

5. If you must jog alone, stay away from unpopulated areas.

Jogging by itself, is not dangerous, but when you add automobiles, animals, reptiles, insects, weather-related conditions, and personal safety measures, sometimes the jogger is put on the defensive. This suggests that joggers need to be defensive runners, just as the National Safety Council urges people to be defensive drivers.

REFERENCES

1. Editors of *Runner's World. The Complete Runner.* Mountain View, California: World Publications, 1974.

2. Editors of *Runner's World. Running After 40.* Mountain View, California: World Publications, 1980.

3. Fisher, A. Garth and Allsen, E. Phillip. *Jogging.* Dubuque, Iowa: Wm. C. Brown, 1980.

4. Geline, Robert J. *The Practical Runner.* New York: Macmillan Publishing Co., Inc., 1978.

5. Henderson, Joe. *Jog, Run, Race.* Mountain View, California: World Publications, 1977.

6. Ullyot, Joan. *Women's Running.* Mountain View, California: World Publications, 1976.

Chapter 10
Injuries

Hopefully, at this point you are convinced of the benefits and pleasure that can result from a planned jogging program. Unfortunately, there is a prevalent myth that to experience the pleasure and values of jogging one must also endure injuries. There is nothing inevitable about getting hurt. What most beginning joggers do not understand is that 80 percent of all jogging injuries can be prevented through knowledge concerning correct jogging technique and progression, proper equipment, and a good ten-minute muscle stretching warm-up prior to working out and a cool-down session afterward. In previous chapters each of these points has been discussed and injury prevention benefits outlined. In this chapter we will present the most common injuries associated with jogging and discuss how to handle them should they occur.

For the past several hundred years many injuries were treated with heat — steaming baths where leisurely soaking was encouraged, hot water bottles, or electric heating pads or wraps. It was assumed that since heat speeded up metabolism, it would also speed the healing process. Today's researchers have proved that just the opposite is true. (5) Heat does speed up body processes but it also stimulates injured tissue and dilates blood vessels. In turn, this causes swelling to increase and enlarges the pools of blood and fluid, actually slowing healing. Even if there is no injury, heat after exercising can cause aches and pains. A quick, cool shower is recommended after your jog rather than a hot tub.

Four basic first aid procedures are used in treating the majority of runners' injuries.

Stop Activity. The first and most critical is to stop jogging as soon as the symptom appears. About the only pain you can run through is a side stitch. Joggers who insist on running with pain or walking off an injury usually incur further harm. Even though the pain does not become more intense, continuing the activity may aggravate the injury and prolong healing.

Apply Cold. Cold packs are now universally accepted as the best first aid for virtually any jogging injury and constitute the second step in treatment. Chilling numbs the pain and minimizes swelling and inflammation by constricting blood and lymph vessels. Apply cold packs at least twice a day until the swelling and tenderness disappear. The ice pack should not be left in place longer than 30 minutes at one time. Muscle cramps are one of the few conditions associated with jogging where heat instead of cold should be applied.

Immobilize and Elevate. Injuries that would benefit from being immobilized and/or given additional support should be wrapped with an elastic Ace-type bandage. This wrapping should be snug, but not tight enough to inhibit blood circulation. This third step should be taken before the final step of elevating the injured body part. Elevation not only helps drain fluid from the area, but also prevents blood and fluid from rushing to the area, thereby causing further swelling.

Blisters

Friction blisters may be caused by poorly-fitting shoes, a wrinkle in a wet or dirty sock, or excessive use of feet that are not calloused. If a blister occurs, probably the best course of action is to relieve the pressure until the fluid is absorbed. However, this often cannot be done. In such cases, thoroughly scrub the part with soap and water, then sterilize a needle by holding it over a match flame and make a small opening at the base of the blister. Drain the fluid and apply a sterile dressing.

The area sometimes can be protected by applying a small felt or rubber pad with a hole (doughnut) cut in the center. This protection, plus taking care of what caused the blister in the first place, can start you jogging again. To prevent blisters, some joggers apply petroleum jelly or powder to their feet and shoes to minimize friction. Clean socks and shoes that fit are a must in the prevention of blisters.

Heel Pain

Heel pain, sometimes called a "stone bruise," usually occurs in the center or outer edge of the fat pad of the heel. The injury occurs because of repeated pounding of the heel on a hard surface, causing a swelling of the bursa lying between the fat pad and the bone of the heel. The best way to prevent this problem is to avoid running on hard surfaces and to wear shoes that are adequately cushioned. Also, ice applied immediately after running will reduce swelling, and a special heel cup will reduce shock to the heel area. This injury does not heal quickly.

Stress Fracture – Foot

A stress fracture is a microscopic break of the long bones (metatarsals) of the foot. Distance runners and others who put prolonged stress on the foot are especially susceptible. The injury causes swelling and needle-like pain, and can only be diagnosed by x-ray. Stress-type fractures can be prevented by the use of a broadsoled running shoe with sufficient cushioning.

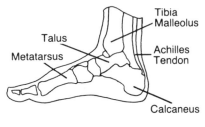

Sprained Ankle

Sprains are injuries to ligaments surrounding a joint or to the capsule-like sac that surrounds a joint. The runner usually sprains the ankle by stepping into an unseen hole. While a severe sprain may not be distinguishable from a more serious fracture except by x-ray, follow the four basic first-aid steps previously discussed for treatment of this condition: stop activity, apply ice, elevate, and immobilize.

Achilles Tendonitis

The Achilles tendon is a cord inside a tube (sheath) connecting the heel to the calf muscle. Achilles tendonitis results when the fluid between the tendon and its sheath expands. Since there is less space for the tendon to move in, the area feels swollen and painful when you pinch along the tendon. The condition usually results if anything pulls too much on either end of the tendon, such as the calf muscle being too short.

Rest is the first and sometimes the only treatment for Achilles tendon aches. A cold pack to the area will relieve the pain and reduce inflammation. Adding a piece of sponge rubber under the heel in your street shoes will help eliminate some of the pulling.

After the healing process has begun and you return to your running schedule, do lots of stretching exercises designed to stretch the heel cord and calf muscle. Also, stay away from uphill running until your calf muscle is again stretched.

Runner's Knee

The medical name for runner's knee is chondromalacia of the patella (*chondro* – cartilage; *malacia* – softening; *patella* – kneecap). The condition is a result of improper mechanical action between the kneecap and the bottom of the thigh bone. Normally, when the heel of a foot lands flat during a run, the kneecap moves smoothly in a pocket between two ridges of the thigh bone. If the foot tilts in (pronates), so do the bones and muscles of the lower leg. As the thigh muscle is stretched outward to compensate, the kneecap is also being pulled outward. The kneecap then begins to grind against the thigh bone, wearing the cartilage on the underside, causing pain on either side of the knee. A number of factors can cause runner's knee, such as weak quadriceps, incorrect footplant (caused by foot structure or shoes), or running on a banked surface.

Runner's knee can be difficult to treat. Placing a cold pack on the knee after running helps numb the pain and reduce inflammation. Long-range cures involve exercises that strengthen the quadriceps and stretch the hamstrings, visiting a podiatrist to have your running style checked, running on a flat surface, or trying a commercially-made foot support.

Muscle Strains

Muscle strains frequently occur to the unconditioned jogger. Such injuries almost always arise from overstressing a tired muscle or making a sudden change in speed — especially when you haven't warmed up properly. An adequate conditioning program decreases the possibility of such injuries.

Most authorities feel the best treatment is the immediate application of cold packs intermittently for up to 24 hours. After 24 – 28 hours most trainers prefer whirlpool baths, ultrasonic, and deep heat treatment. These injuries are very slow to heal and require much reconditioning.

Shin Splints

It is usually best to run on soft surfaces, such as grass, as this reduces the stress on joints and connective tissue. Proper footwear will greatly aid in absorbing the shock of running.

Prolonged running on hard surfaces or toes (improper foot plant) sometimes causes an inflammation and microscopic tearing of the muscles and tendons of the lower leg. This condition, commonly called "shin splints," usually responds best to complete rest of the legs, ice packs, compression and elevation. After the pain has subsided, strengthen the calf muscles before resuming jogging and do not run on your toes.

Pulled Hamstrings

Damage to the hamstring muscles, which are located at the back of the thighs, often occurs when trying to run at full speed. First aid for such an injury consists of ice packs, elevation, a firm bandage (Ace) and rest. Warm applications, gentle massage and exercise are generally applied after the ruptured muscles have healed.

Thigh Bruises

Such injuries frequently result in some bleeding within the muscle. In time this blood is absorbed by the body with little apparent after-effect. However, sometimes calcium deposits and scar tissue may develop. If this complication occurs it may result in shortening within the muscle and pain where the muscle is stretched. Bruises should be treated with immediate cold, elevation, firm support (Ace bandages) and rest.

Cramps

Muscle spasms, or cramps, are sudden, violent, involuntary muscle contractions that can be excruciatingly painful. Cramps may occur while engaging in activity or may occur during rest or sleep. There are two distinct types of cramping. The clonic type is characterized by repeated contractions and relaxation of the muscles, while the tonic type is continuous and. steady contraction.

The cause of cramps is sometimes difficult to determine. However, the onset of fatigue, depletion of body fluids and minerals, loss of reciprocal muscle coordination are all contributing factors.

When a cramp occurs in the body, the best thing to do is to stop immediately and alleviate the spasm by the application of constant pressure. Should it occur in the leg or foot, sometimes just putting body weight on the limb will help. When the cramp has dissipated, an easy gradual stretch of the body part affected will usually help. Moist warm heat will also assist in relaxing muscles.

Muscle Soreness

Unfortunately one of the universal outcomes of vigorous exercise is muscle soreness. This is particularly true when the exercise occurs after a prolonged period of inactivity. Although the causes of muscle soreness are not yet fully understood, some researchers believe that an over-accumulation of lactic acid in the tissues, brought about by fatigue, somehow triggers the pain symptom. Another factor is the accumulation of lactic acid in the affected muscle which causes pressure on nerve endings. Another hypothesis by DeVries (3) indicates that muscle soreness may be caused by "tonic muscle spasms," i.e. small, continuous muscle contractions.

Limited activity in the form of gently stretching and usage is probably the best means of dispelling the symptoms. However, gentle massage and warm baths seem to give some relief, although the effects may be more psychological than physiological.

Back Pain

One of the leading problems plaguing weekend joggers is that of back pain. The most common causes of back pain are weak abdominal muscles and tight hamstring and back muscles.

The treatment of most back problems involves bed rest on a very firm mattress (usually with boards underneath), limited heat (no more than 30 minutes per sitting and no more than four times in a 24-hour stretch), gentle traction (such as hanging from a chinning bar or door sill) and exercises to strengthen the muscles involved. Of course, if there is damage to the vertebrae or their discs, medical attention is a necessity.

"Inversion Boots," a recent innovation which allows a person to safely hang head down from a chinning bar, seems to have some promise in the treatment of certain back problems.

Side Stitches

A "stitch" may develop in individuals who are beginning a jogging program. It is a rather sharp pain, usually located on the upper right side, just under the ribs. While the cause is unknown, there are a number of theories:

1. Reduced blood flow to the area due to demands elsewhere in the body.

2. Accumulation of lactic acid in the diaphragm.

3. Diaphragm spasm produced by faulty breathing.

4. Formation of gas in the ascending colon

Trained individuals rarely experience the pain. Abdominal breathing during the run and large arm-circles prior to the run may prevent the pain from occurring. If the pain does occur, relief may be obtained by applying pressure on the affected side while continuing the jog, or stretching in the opposite direction. If the pain continues, the only alternatives are to slow down or stop altogether.

Heat Exhaustion

Heat exhaustion is a reponse to heat characterized by fatigue, weakness, and collapse due to inadequate intake of fluids to compensate for loss of body salts nd fluids through sweating. Heat exhaustion symptoms are pale skin, profuse erspiration, nausea, and frequent urination with body temperature normal. First id measures include moving the victim to a cool area and protection from chilling; dministering a salt solution of a half-teaspoon of salt per half-glass of water very 15 minutes for three or four doses; and bed rest.

Heat Stroke

Heat stroke is a response to heat characterized by extremely high body temperature and disturbance of the body's cooling mechanism. Heat stroke symptoms are hot, dry skin, high body temperature, very rapid pulse, and frequent unconsciousness. First aid measures include cooling the victim with cold water and prompt removal to a hospital.

REFERENCES

1. American Academy of Orthopedic Surgeons. *Emergency Care and Transportation of the Sick and Injured.* George Bantam Co., 1971.

2. Arnheim, Daniel D. *Dance Injuries.* St. Louis: C. V. Mosby and Company, 1975.

3. DeVries, Herbert A. *Physiology of Exercise.* Dubuque, Iowa: Wm. C. Brown, 1970.

4. Dominaquez, Richard H. *The Complete Book of Sports Medicine.* New York: Scribner Sons, 1979.

5. Kalenak, Alexander, et al. "Athletic Injuries: Heat vs. Cold." *American Family Physician,* November, 1975.

6. Schneider, Myles. "Everything You Need to Know About Staying One Step Ahead of Foot Problems." *Runner's World.* November, 1981, pp. 28-33.

7. Stokes, Roberta; Moore, A.; Moore, C.; and Williams, C. *Fitness: The New Wave.* Winston-Salem, North Carolina: Hunter Textbooks Inc., 1981.

8. The American National Red Cross. *Advanced First Aid and Emergency Care,* 1973.

9. Weisenfeld, Murray F. with Burr, Barbara. *The Runner's Repair Manual.* New York: St. Martin's Press, 1980.

Chapter 11
The Jogger's Diet

Do we eat to live, or live to eat? By the appearance of approximately 30 million overweight Americans it would seem the latter is true for many. However, the major reason for eating is to provide the body with the basic chemicals it needs for carrying on the processes of life.

Athletes at all levels are concerned about eating foods that maximize performance. Numerous myths, rituals, and diet fads are guilty of omitting basic nutritional essentials. In an attempt to acquire additional energy and endurance, athletes have stuffed themselves with vitamins, mineral supplements, protein pills, wheat germ, bee pollen and a host of other additives. **There is no research to prove that any of these can improve physical performance.**

As with other athletes, joggers need to eat a variety of foods, since there are really no "miracle foods" that can supply the body with all of the nutrients it needs.

Food scientists tell us that about fifty known nutrients plus water are necessary for us to live and be healthy. Nutrients are essential for the body to build and maintain body cells, to regulate body processes, and to supply energy. The basic nutrients are protein, carbohydrates, fats, vitamins, and minerals.

In order to obtain an adequate supply of the nutrients needed by the body, a balanced diet is required. What is a balanced diet? A balanced diet means eating the proper foods in the proper amounts. Nutritionists have grouped foods into four categories for ease in planning daily food intake to insure a balanced diet. Most foods fit into one of these categories called the Basic Four Food Groups.

Meat Group

Foods in the meat group comprise protein-rich foods, sources of iron and certain B vitamins. We should eat two or more servings a day of foods from this group. A serving is counted as 2-3 ounces of cooked lean meat, discounting bones or fat. For example, 2 slices of roast beef, 1 hamburger patty (3" x ½"), 1 thick chop, one chicken leg or thigh, half a small chicken breast, 4 fish sticks, ¾ cup (c.) oysters, or 2 eggs constitute one serving. These foods furnish the best source of protein or "complete protein," since they contain adequate amounts of all essential amino acids. Incomplete protein, on the other hand, is lacking in one or more essential amino acids. Perhaps the easiest way to remember the difference between complete and incomplete protein foods is to think of the food source. Animal sources provide complete protein and plant sources incomplete protein. For meal variety, or for the vegetarian, these incomplete protein foods constitute a serving from the Meat Group: 1 c. of dried cooked peas, beans, or lentils; ½ c. nuts; ⅓ c. peanuts; ¼ c. peanut butter.

Foods Included In The Meat Group:

Pork	Lamb	Fish	Dried Peas and Beans
Beef	Turkey	Eggs	Peanut Butter
Veal	Chicken	Shellfish	Nuts

Fruit and Vegetable Group

This food group contains all fruits and vegetables and is one of best sources of vitamins A and C. Four or more servings a day are required for good nutrition. A good food source of Vitamin C (citrus fruit or juice) should be included as one of these four servings daily, since Vitamin C cannot be readily stored in the body.

Every other day a good food source of Vitamin A (dark green or deep yellow vegetables) should be eaten. One serving is equal to: one medium fruit — orange, apple, banana; 10-12 grapes; 1 c. fresh berries, ½ c. fruit juice; ½ c cooked vegetables; or 1 c. raw leafy vegetables.

Eating raw fruits and vegetables insures that the nutrients they contain are left intact. However, if fruits and vegetables are cooked, they should be cooked quickly in a small amount of water to conserve food value. Water soluble vitamins are especially sensitive to heat. Many nutritionists claim that the kitchen sink is probably better nourished than many adults, since the liquid from most cooked foods usually ends up there.

Fruit and Vegetable Group Foods:

Broccoli*	Apple	Turnip Greens*	Carrots*
Green Beans	Banana	Cantaloupe**	Corn
Grapefruit**	Sweet Potatoes*	Strawberries**	Tomatoes**

*good source of Vitamin A   **good source of Vitamin C

Bread and Cereal Group

The bread and cereal group is a good source for carbohydrates, iron, and B vitamins. When buying these products, look for ones that are labeled enriched, restored, or fortified, since many of the B vitamins are lost during the milling process of grains. Four or more servings a day should be eaten from this group. One serving equals: 1 c. ready-to-eat cereal; ½-¾ c. cooked cereal, grits, rice or pasta; 1 slice bread; 1 roll, biscuit, or muffin; 1 pancake, waffle, popover, or bagel 6 graham crackers; 1 doughnut, 1 wedge pizza crust.

Bread and Cereal Group Foods:

Cornbread	Spaghetti	Muffin	Hot Dog Bun
Grits	Macaroni	Wheat Germ	Crackers
Frosted Flakes	Tortillas	Waffle	Oatmeal

Milk Group

Milk and dairy products are included in this group and are excellent sources of calcium, phosphorus, protein, and riboflavin. Buy milk that has been fortified with vitamins A and D. This is especially important if you buy low fat milk.

Our daily needs for milk vary according to age and special conditions. Teenagers need four 8-ounce cups, while adults need two 8-ounce cups daily. If you are not a milk drinker, other dairy products may be eaten to receive the same nutritional benefits. The following equivalents are based on the calcium content of one cup of milk: 1 c. plain yogurt; ½ c. ice cream; 1 c. baked custard; ½ c. pudding; 1 oz. slice Swiss cheese; 2 oz. slice American cheese; ½ c. creamed cottage cheese.

Milk Group Foods:

Milk Shake	Ice Cream	Buttermilk	Yogurt
Cottage Cheese	Cream	Pudding	Swiss cheese
			Cream cheese

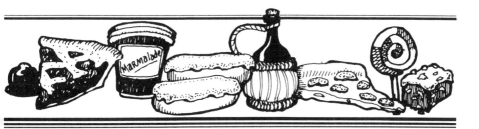

The Fifth Dimension

After reading this section on the Basic Four you are probably wondering where some of the other "food stuffs" that add flavor and variety to meals belong. Some nutritionists call this the fifth dimension. While butter, salad dressings, dips, gravies, sauces, candies, jam, jellies, alcoholic and carbonated beverages may be enjoyable, they do not provide enough nutrients to be categorized in the Basic Four. Their major contribution is in the form of calories, and when it is time to cut back, these should be the first to go.

Water

In additon to eating a balanced diet, two to three quarts of water should be taken daily. Although water carries no food value, it assists in the digestion of food, excretion, glandular secretion, and in the forming of blood plasma.

Water is the only nutrient of greater importance to the jogger than to the nonjogger, especially during prolonged training periods carried out in a hot, humid environment. During jogging, the largest amount of water is lost through the skin. It is extremely difficult to replace the water as it is lost, but partial replacement can prevent overheating and dehydration.

Drink plenty of liquids before, during and after exercising.

CALORIE — A UNIT OF POTENTIAL ENERGY

When selecting foods from the Basic Four Food Groups, please be calorie conscious. All foods contain calories, but the amount varies from food to food within the groups and is somewhat dependent on the method of preparation. For example, fried foods are usually higher in calories than the same foods broiled.

A calorie is the unit of measurement used to express the potential energy of food and the amount of energy used by the body in performing various activities. The energy level required to keep the body functioning is influenced by body composition, body size, and age. Generally, men have a higher minimum caloric need than women due to a greater proportion of muscle to adipose tissue.

The body uses energy constantly, and even the most sedentary person needs some energy everyday. Even while resting, we need energy for the basic functions of breathing and circulation of blood. Energy is also required to maintain body temperature, nerve function, and growth and repair of body tissue. During strenuous exercise 10-15 times as many calories are required for the muscular contractions that occur.

When you consume more calories than you burn, the excess calories are stored in the body as fat. However, if you burn more calories than you eat, stored reserves are utilized to maintain body functions. Calling on these reserves over a period of time will result in a loss of weight. In order to maintain weight, calorie expenditure (output) must equal calorie intake (input) over the long run.

Overweight vs Obesity

We have all heard the adage, "The way to a man's heart is through his stomach." This may be truer than people realize since there is a close association between excess weight and heart attacks. In fact, life insurance companies have long considered overweight individuals poor risks. A primary reason for the close association between overweight and cardiovascular disease is the increased strain that excess body weight places on the heart and circulatory system. As body fat increases so does the body surface area, requiring an expansion of arteries, veins, and capillaries to serve the larger area. It is often said that 20 pounds of fat means 20 miles of capillaries. This, of course, places a much greater work load on the heart, forcing it to continually pump blood through a greatly expanded vasuclar system.

An overweight individual is generally defined as one who weighs more than 10 percent above desirable level. Public health records indicate such individuals make up 40 to 50 percent of the United States population.

The easiest and most common method for determining whether one is overweight is to refer to a standardized height-weight chart. However, care must be taken to select one that is based on adequate research and allows for differences in body type as well as height. Avoid tables which allow for increased body weight as one ages. As individuals grow older, they become less active. This reduction in activity, along with a decline in the basal metabolism rate, means that eating habits must adjust to the aging process. Otherwise, gains or increases in body fat percentages will occur. It is not uncommon for people at age fifty to weigh the same as when they were actively involved in sports in college, but still be obese. What happened is that the muscles have atrophied and the percentage of fat has increased.

A more accurate method of determining desired body weight is to calculate it on the basis of fat weight and desired percentage of body fat. This is accomplished by pinching a fold of skin between the thumb and forefinger and measuring with a skinfold caliper. An obese person is one who has an excess accumulation of body fat. An acceptable percentage of body fat for the average person is estimated to be 10-15 percent for men and 15-20 percent for women. See Laboratory C-4 for the appropriate formula to estimate percentage of body fat.

Using these guidelines, one could be obese without being overweight or could be overweight without being obese. It is not so much a question of how much a person weighs, but how much excess body fat they carry that affects one's health.

Weight Control

Excess calories add up day by day and month by month. One does not become obese overnight, but over a period of time. Nutritionists refer to this as "creeping obesity." *One hundred calories per day beyond expenditure over a one-year*

TABLE 8
DESIRABLE WEIGHTS FOR MEN

Weights listed without clothing according to height without shoes. (From U.S. Department of Agriculture, *Food and Your Weight*, Washington, D.C.: U.S. Government Printing Office, 1973)

Height (feet, inches)	Weight (lbs.)		
	Below Average	Average	Above Average
5 - 3	118	129	141
5 - 4	122	133	145
5 - 5	126	137	149
5 - 6	130	142	155
5 - 7	134	147	161
5 - 8	139	151	166
5 - 9	143	155	170
5 - 10	147	159	174
5 - 11	150	163	178
6 - 0	154	167	183
6 - 1	158	171	188
6 - 2	162	175	192
6 - 3	165	178	195

TABLE 9
DESIRABLE WEIGHTS FOR WOMEN

Weights listed without clothing according to height without shoes. (From U.S. Department of Agriculture, *Food and Your Weight*, Washington D.C.: U.S. Government Printing Office, 1973)

Height (feet, inches)	Weight (lbs.)		
	Below Average	Average	Above Average
5 - 0	100	109	118
5 - 1	104	112	121
5 - 2	107	115	125
5 - 3	110	118	128
5 - 4	113	122	132
5 - 5	116	125	135
5 - 6	120	129	139
5 - 7	123	132	142
5 - 8	126	136	146
5 - 9	130	140	151
5 - 10	133	144	156
5 - 11	137	148	161
6 - 0	141	152	166

period results in a weight gain of ten pounds. For women, this translates to one dress size larger. Over a five-year span the size "creeps" from a size 6 to a size 14.

In order to lose one pound per week, daily caloric intake should be decreased by 500 calories or 3,500 calories per week. Since 40 percent of the calories in the typical American diet is from fat, this may be one area of the diet that can be cut back. A reduction in fatty foods such as butter, margarine, bacon, sausage, fried foods, salad dressing, whole milk and red meat will add to saved calories. However, it is important that these foods not be eliminated entirely from the diet.

Many experts advocate low carbohydrate diets. If you are eating two slices of toast for breakfast, a sandwich for lunch (2 pieces of bread), 2 muffins for dinner and 3 cookies before bedtime, you would be wise to cut down on the carbohydrate foods — but not cut out entirely. The best diet is one that limits calories, while maintaining a balanced combination of protein, carbohydrate, and fat. It is very easy to accumulate extra inches if the most vigorous physical activity you participate in is eating.

There is a widely held myth that exercise does little to reduce weight. Individuals who propose this belief state that it takes 11½ hours of walking, 5½ hours of swimming, or 3½ hours of jogging to lose one pound of fat. They always draw a mental picture of the exercise being done in one long session. (1)

Weight loss occurs whether the exercise is performed during one long session or for a few minutes spread over a period of weeks. For example, jogging 3½ hours to burn up 3,500 calories, or lose one pound, would totally exhaust the average person. A more appropriate approach would be to jog for twenty minutes (200 caloric expenditure per session) seven days a week, which would add up to the required expenditure in two and a half weeks. In one year, you could shed over 20 pounds of body fat. On the other hand, if eating is one of your hobbies, you might not lose weight but jogging would prevent your adding the 20 pounds as fat. (2)

The most effective strategy for a lifetime of successful weight control is a sound, nutritious diet combined with regular vigorous exercise. Many people try to lose weight by exercising only, while others attempt eating reduced amounts of food only. If you lose weight by diet only, muscle mass is lost at the same time. That is one of the reasons why obese people, who lose weight through diet alone, often look flabby. It is important to realize that those who exercise and diet tend to lose a much greater portion of fat. Despite what many people think, exercise does not increase your appetite, but often serves to suppress it.

The American Medical Association states, "It usually is unwise to try to lose more than two pounds per week because rapid weight loss may leave a person

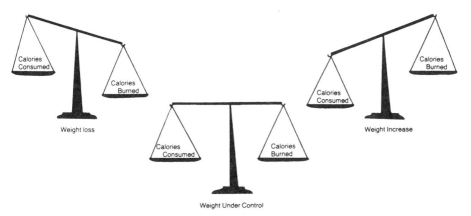

TABLE 10
CALORIES BURNED WHILE JOGGING

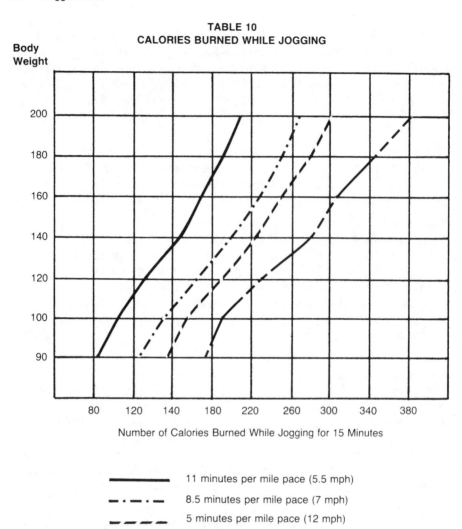

Number of Calories Burned While Jogging for 15 Minutes

————————	11 minutes per mile pace (5.5 mph)
— . — . —	8.5 minutes per mile pace (7 mph)
— — — —	5 minutes per mile pace (12 mph)
— — — —	4 minutes per mile pace (9 mph)

tired, grumpy and vulnerable to illness." A diet requiring large cutbacks in the food you normally eat is difficult to maintain, since you may feel deprived and are tempted to forget the whole thing.

To be effective, diets must be considered from a long-range view and must result in the adoption of a lifetime style of eating that can be lived with every day. Unfortunately, "fad diets" do not follow good dietary concepts. Some may lead to long-term health problems and others have caused deaths. Since fad dieting does not recognize that losing weight is a permanent long-term problem, most weight loss from such diets is usually temporary.

Obviously we are creatures of what we eat, but we are also creatures of what we fail to eat. In order to maintain optimal health, we must provide our bodies with the right food in sufficient amounts. Whether at work, in school, in sports or in leisure activities, we can perform only as well as our physical well being allows. Through better nutrition all of life's qualities can be improved.

REFERENCES

1. Berland, Theodore. "The Diet Connection." *Insider*. Fall, 1978, pp. 10-15.

2. Fisher, A. Garth and Conlee, Robert. *The Complete Book of Physical Fitness*. Salt Lake City: Brigham Young University Press, 1979.

3. General Mills Nutrition Department. "Energy for Sport."

4. General Mills Nutrition Department. "Nutrition — An Essential for Health."

5. Getchell, Bud. *Physical Fitness: A Way of Life*. New York: John Wiley and Sons, Inc., 1976.

6. Leveille, G. A. and Rosmos, D. R. "Meal Eating and Obesity." *Nutrition Today*, 1974, pp. 4-9.

7. Stokes, Roberta; Moore A.; Moore, C.; and Williams, C. *Fitness: The New Wave*. Winston-Salem, North Carolina: Hunter Textbooks Inc., 1981.

Appendices

APPENDIX A

SIXTEEN-WEEK BEGINNING JOGGING PROGRAM FOR INDIVIDUALS UNDER 30 YEARS OF AGE

The following sixteen-week jogging program is an adaptation from the President's Council on Physical Fitness and Sport and is offered as a guide. It is understood that individuals with an average or advanced fitness level will need to enter the program in its latter states (i.e., week 12 or 14), while those who scored in the lower categories will need to begin with week one. Regardless of your fitness classification, if after taking a fitness test you suffered from extremely sore muscles, nausea, fatigue, dizziness or a slow recovery heart rate, you would be wise to be conservative in selecting the entry point of the program.

Remember to monitor your resting, training and recovery heart rate. The resting heart rate is needed to compute your target zone. If while training your heart rate goes above or below the intensity at which you wish to train, adjustments need to be made. Additionally, if after five minutes your recovery heart rate is not less than 120 beats per minute (B.P.M.) or lower than 100 B.P.M. ten minutes after jogging, you need to reduce the intensity or duration of the jog.

After completing the sixteen-week program, your legs and cardiovascular system should be in good physical condition. You will have the foundation which will help you to enjoy a happy, productive, worthwhile and enjoyable way of living. To maintain this level of fitness, continue the program as prescribed in weeks 14, 15, or 16 by gradually increasing the intensity, duration and/or frequency of your training program.

DISTANCE EQUIVALENTS TABLE

| Yards | Imperial | | Metric |
	Miles		Meters
	fraction	decimal	
110	1/16	.06	100.58
220	1/8	.13	201.17
440	1/4	.25	402.34
660	3/8	.38	603.50
880	1/2	.50	804.67
1,100	5/8	.63	1,005.84
1,320	3/4	.75	1,207.01
1.540	7/8	.88	1,409.18
1,760	1	1.00	1,609.34

*For distances longer than one mile use the appropriate multiplier.

WALK-JOG-RUN PACE CHART

Pace	Speed (MPH)	55 yds.	110 yds.	220 yds.	440 yds.	880 yds.	1 mile
				Time for Various Distances (min:sec)			
Slow Walk	3	:38	1:15	2:30	5:00	10:00	20:00
Moderate Walk	4	:28	:56	1:52	3:45	7:30	15:00
Fast Walk	4.5	:25	:50	1:40	3:20	6:40	13:20
Slow Jog	5	:22	:45	1:30	3:00	6:00	12:00
Moderate Jog	6	:19	:38	1:15	2:30	5:00	10:00
Fast Jog	7	:17	:33	1:05	2:09	4:17	8:34
Slow Run	8	:15	:29	:57	1:54	3:47	7:34
Moderate Run	9	:13	:25	:50	1:40	3:20	6:40
Fast Run	10	:11	:22	:45	1:30	3:00	6:00
Competitive Running	11	:10.5	:21	:41	1:22	2:44	5:27
	12	:9.5	:19	:38	1:15	2:30	5:00
	15	:7.5	:15	:30	1:00	2:00	4:00

This chart should be used to help you follow the basic jogging program provided here or any other exercise program that involves walking, jogging or running. If you know the distance you are walking, jogging or running, you can time yourself over these distances to determine your pace.

SUMMARY OF SIXTEEN WEEK BEGINNING JOGGING PROGRAM BY FITNESS CATEGORY

Very Poor Category

Week	Distance*(miles)	Duration (min.)	Intensity	Frequency/wk.
1	1/8	1:30	50%	3
2	1/4	3:00	55%	3
3	1/2	6:00	60%	3
4	3/4	9:00	60%	3
5	3/4	7:30	65%	4
6	1	12:00	65%	4

Poor Category — Begin program with the routine listed for the 7th week.

7	1	12:00	65%	5
8	1 1/8	13:30	70%	5
9	1 1/4	15:00	70%	5
10	1 1/4	12:30	75%	5

Fair Category — Begin program with the routine listed for the 11th week. If not sure, reduce your starting program to a week listed above that you can comfortably handle.

11	1 1/2	18:00	70-80%	5
12	1 3/4	21:00	70-80%	5
13	2	24:00	70-80%	5
14	2 1/4	27:00	70-85%	5
15	2 1/2	30:00	70-85%	5
16	3	40:00	70-85%	5

*Walking should be added to distance for the warm-up and cool-down. It is best to add additional walking during the initial stages.

DAILY JOGGING PROGRAM

WEEK 1*

Day 1	Flexibility Exercises					15:00 min.
	Walk	880	yds.	(½ mile)	moderate pace	7-8:00 min.
	Jog	110	yds.	(1/16 mile)	slow pace	45 sec.
	Walk	220	yds.	(⅛ mile)	slow pace	2:30 min.
Day 2	Flexibility Exercises					15:00 min.
	Walk	880	yds.	(½ mile)	moderate pace	7-8:00 min.
Day 3	Repeat Day 1					
Day 4	Repeat Day 2					
Day 5	Flexibility Exercises					15:00 min.
	Walk	880	yds.	(½ mile)	moderate pace	7-8:00 min.
	Jog	220	yds.	(⅛ mile)	moderate pace	1:15 min.
	Walk	440	yds.	(¼ mile)	slow pace	5:00 min.

WEEK 2

Day 1	Walk	440	yds.	(¼ mile)	moderate pace	3:45 min.
	Jog	220	yds.	(⅛ mile)	slow pace	1:30 min.
	Walk	220	yds.	(⅛ mile)	moderate pace	1:52 min.
	Jog	220	yds.	(⅛ mile)	slow pace	1:30 min.
	Walk	440	yds.	(¼ mile)	slow pace	5:00 min.
Day 2	Walk	880	yds.	(½ mile)	slow pace	10:00 min.
Day 3	Walk	440	yds.	(¼ mile)	moderate pace	3:45 min.
	Jog	440	yds.	(¼ mile)	slow pace	3:00 min.
	Walk	440	yds.	(¼ mile)	moderate pace	3:45 min.
Day 4	Repeat Day 2					
Day 5	Walk	440	yds.	(¼ mile)	moderate pace	3:45 min.
	Jog	660	yds.	(⅜ mile)	slow pace	4:30 min.
	Walk	220	yds.	(⅛ mile)	moderate pace	1:52 min.

WEEK 3

Day 1	Walk	440	yds.	(¼ mile)	moderate pace	3:45 min.
	Jog	660	yds.	(⅜ mile)	slow pace	4:30 min.
	Walk	440	yds.	(¼ mile)	moderate pace	3:45 min.
Day 2	Walk	1760	yds.	(1 mile)	moderate pace	15:00 min.
Day 3	Walk	440	yds.	(¼ mile)	moderate pace	3:45 min.
	Jog	660	yds.	(⅜ mile)	moderate pace ·	3:45 min.
	Walk	440	yds.	(¼ mile	moderate pace	3:45 min.

*Emphasis on stretching exercises and correct foot placement.

Day 4   Repeat Day 2

Day 5	Walk	440 yds.	(¼ mile)	moderate pace	3:45 min.
	Jog	880 yds.	(½ mile)	slow pace	6:00 min.
	Walk	220 yds.	(⅛ mile)	slow pace	2:30 min.

WEEK 4

Day 1	Walk	440 yds.	(¼ mile)	moderate pace	3:45 min.
	Jog	440 yds.	(¼ mile)	fast pace	1:05 min.
	Walk	220 yds.	(⅛ mile)	moderate pace	1:52 min.
	Jog	440 yds.	(¼ mile	fast pace	1:05 min.
	Walk	440 yds.	(¼ mile)	moderate pace	3:45 min.

| Day 2 | Walk | 1760 yds. | (1 mile) | moderate pace | 15:00 min. |

Day 3	Walk	440 yds.	(¼ mile)	moderate pace	3:45 min.
	Jog	880 yds.	(½ mile)	moderate pace	5:00 min.
	Walk	440 yds.	(¼ mile)	moderate pace	3:45 min.

Day 4   Same as Day 2

Day 5	Walk	440 yds.	(¼ mile)	moderate pace	3:45 min.
	Jog	1100 yds.	(⅝ mile)	moderate pace	6:15 min.
	Walk	220 yds.	(⅛ mile)	moderate pace	1:52 min.

WEEK 5

Day 1	Walk	440 yds.	(¼ mile)	brisk pace	3:20 min.
	Jog	1100 yds.	(⅝ mile)	moderate pace	6:15 min.
	Walk	440 yds.	(¼ mile)	moderate pace	3:45 min.

Day 2   Repeat Day 1

Day 3	Walk	440 yds.	(¼ mile)	brisk pace	3:20 min.
	Jog	1100 yds.	(⅝ mile)	brisk pace	5:22 min.
	Walk	660 yds.	(⅜ mile)	moderate pace	5:37 min.

Day 4	Walk	440 yds.	(¼ mile)	brisk pace	3:20 min.
	Jog	1100 yds.	(⅝ mile)	brisk pace	5:22 min.
	Walk	660 yds.	(⅜ mile)	brisk pace	5:00 min.

Day 5	Walk	440 yds.	(¼ mile)	brisk pace	3:20 min.
	Jog	1320 yds.	(¾ mile)	moderate pace	7:30 min.
	Walk	220 yds.	(⅛ mile)	moderate pace	1:52 min.

WEEK 6

Day 1	Walk	440 yds.	(¼ mile)	brisk pace	3:20 min.
	Jog	1320 yds.	(¾ mile)	moderate pace	7:30 min.
	Walk	440 yds.	(¼ mile)	moderate pace	3:45 min.

Day 2	Walk	440	yds.	(¼ mile)	brisk pace	3:20 min.
	Jog	1320	yds.	(¾ mile)	moderate pace	7:30 min.
	Walk	660	yds.	(⅜ mile)	moderate pace	5:37 min.
Day 3	Repeat Day 2					
Day 4	Walk	440	yds.	(¼ mile)	brisk pace	3:20 min.
	Jog	1320	yds.	(¾ mile)	moderate pace	7:30 min.
	Walk	660	yds.	(⅜ mile)	brisk pace	5:00 min.
Day 5	Walk	440	yds.	(¼ mile)	brisk pace	3:20 min.
	Jog	1540	yds.	(⅞ mile)	moderate pace	8:45 min.
	Walk	220	yds.	(⅛ mile)	moderate pace	1:52 min.

WEEK 7

Day 1	Walk	440	yds.	(¼ mile)	brisk pace	3:20 min.
	Jog	1540	yds.	(⅞ mile)	moderate pace	8:45 min.
	Walk	220	yds.	(⅛ mile)	brisk pace	1:40 min.
Day 2	Walk	440	yds.	(¼ mile)	brisk pace	3:20 min.
	Jog	1540	yds.	(⅞ mile)	moderate pace	8:45 min.
	Walk	440	yds.	(¼ mile)	moderate pace	3:45 min.
Day 3	Walk	440	yds.	(¼ mile)	brisk pace	3:20 min.
	Jog	110	yds.		Walk 110 yds.	4 times
	Jog	330	yds.		Walk 330 yds.	
	Jog	220	yds.		Walk 220 yds.	3 times
Day 4	Repeat Day 2					
Day 5	Walk	440	yds.	(¼ mile)	brisk pace	3:20 min.
	Jog	1760	yds.	(1 mile)	slow pace	12:00 min.
	Walk	220	yds.	(⅛ mile)	slow pace	2:30 min.

WEEK 8

Day 1	Walk	440	yds.	(¼ mile)	brisk pace	3:20 min.
	Jog	1760	yds.	(1 mile)	slow pace	12:00 min.
	Walk	440	yds.	(¼ mile)	moderate pace	3:45 min.
Day 2	Walk	440	yds.	(¼ mile)	brisk pace	3:20 min.
	Jog	1760	yds.	(1 mile)	slow pace	12:00 min.
	Walk	660	yds.	(⅜ mile)	moderate pace	5:37 min.
Day 3	Walk	440	yds.	(¼ mile)	brisk pace	3:20 min.
	Jog	1760	yds.	(1 mile)	moderate pace	10:00 min.
	Walk	440	yds.	(¼ mile)	moderate pace	3:45 min.
Day 4	Walk	440	yds.	(¼ mile)	brisk pace	3:20 min.
	Jog	1760	yds.	(1 mile)	moderate pace	10:00 min.
	Jog	110	yds.		Walk 110 yds.	2 times

Day 5	Walk	440	yds.	(¼ mile)	brisk pace	3:20 min.
	Jog	1980	yds.	(1⅛ mile)	slow pace	13:15 min.
	Walk	220	yds.	(⅛ mile)	moderate pace	1:52 min.

WEEK 9

Day 1	Walk	440	yds.	(¼ mile)	brisk pace	3:20 min.
	Jog	1980	yds.	(1⅛ mile)	slow pace	13:15 min.
	Walk	440	yds.	(¼ mile)	moderate pace	3:45 min.
Day 2	Walk	440	yds.	(¼ mile)	brisk pace	3:20 min.
	Jog	1980	yds.	(1⅛ mile)	moderate pace	11:15 min.
	Walk	440	yds.	(¼ mile)	moderate pace	3:45 min.
Day 3	Same as Day 2					
Day 4	Walk	440	yds.	(¼ mile)	brisk pace	3:20 min.
	Jog	1980	yds.	(1⅛ mile)	moderate pace	11:15 min.
	Walk	660	yds.	(⅜ mile)	moderate pace	5:37 min.
Day 5	Walk	440	yds.	(¼ mile)	brisk pace	3:20 min.
	Jog	1760	yds.	(1 mile)	moderate pace	10:00 min.
	Jog	220	yds.		Walk 110 yds.	2 times

WEEK 10

Day 1	Walk	440	yds.	(¼ mile)	brisk pace	3:20 min.
	Jog	2200	yds.	(1¼ mile)	slow pace	15:00 min.
	Walk	220	yds.	(⅛ mile)	slow pace	2:30 min.
Day 2	Repeat Day 1					
Day 3	Walk	440	yds.	(¼ mile)	brisk pace	3:20 min.
	Jog	2200	yds.	(1¼ mile)	moderate pace	12:30 min.
	Walk	440	yds.	(¼ mile)	slow pace	3:45 min.
Day 4	Walk	440	yds.	(¼ mile)	brisk pace	3:20 min.
	Jog	2200	yds.	(1¼ mile)	moderate pace	12:30 min.
	Walk	660	yds.	(⅜ mile)	moderate pace	5:00 min.
Day 5	Walk	440	yds.	(¼ mile)	brisk pace	3:20 min.
	Jog	2420	yds.	(1⅜ mile)	vary pace and walk if necessary	13-17 min.

WEEK 11

Day 1	Walk	440	yds.	(¼ mile)	brisk pace	3:20 min.
	Jog	110	yds.	(1/16 mile)	Walk 55 yds.	4 times
	Jog	220	yds.	(⅛ mile)	Walk 110 yds.	3 times
	Jog	440	yds.	(¼ mile)	Walk 220 yds.	2 times
Day 2	Walk	440	yds.	(¼ mile)	brisk pace	3:20 min.
	Jog	2420	yds.	(1⅜ mile)	moderate pace	14:00 min.
	Walk	440	yds.	(¼ mile)	moderate pace	3:45 min.

Day 3	Walk	440	yds.	(¼ mile)	brisk pace	3:20 min.
	Jog	880	yds.	(½ mile)	Walk 110 yds.	2 times
	Jog	440	yds.	(¼ mile)	Walk 220 yds.	
Day 4	Repeat Day 2					
Day 5	Walk	440	yds.	(¼ mile)	brisk pace	3:20 min.
	Jog	2640	yds.	(1½ mile)	at your own pace	15-18 min.

WEEK 12

Day 1	Walk	440	yds.	(¼ mile)	brisk pace	3:20 min.
	Jog	2640	yds.	(1½ mile)	walk as necessary	15-18 min.
	Walk	220	yds.	(⅛ mile)	moderate pace	1:52 min.
Day 2	Walk	440	yds.	(¼ mile)	brisk pace	3:20 min.
	Jog	2640	yds.	(1½ mile)	walk as necessary	15-18 min.
	Walk	440	yds.	(¼ mile)	moderate pace	3:45 min.
Day 3	Repeat Day 2					
Day 4	Walk	440	yds.	(¼ mile)	brisk pace	3:20 min.
	Jog	440	yds.	(¼ mile)	walk as necessary	2 times
	Jog	220	yds.	(⅛ mile)	walk as necessary	4 times
	Jog	880	yds.	(½ mile)	Walk 220 yds.	
Day 5	Walk	440	yds.	(¼ mile)	brisk pace	3:20 min.
	Jog	3080	yds.	(1¾ mile)	walk as necessary	17-21 min.
	Walk	220	yds.	(⅛ mile)	slow pace	2:30 min.

WEEK 13

Day 1	Walk	440	yds.	(¼ mile)	brisk pace	3:20 min.
	Jog	3080	yds.	(1¾ mile)	moderate pace	18:00 min.
	Walk	440	yds.	(¼ mile)	slow pace	3:45 min.
Day 2	Walk	440	yds.	(¼ mile)	brisk pace	3:20 min.
	Jog	3080	yds.	(1¾ mile)	moderate pace	18:00 min.
	Walk	660	yds.	(⅜ mile)	moderate pace	5:00 min.
Day 3	Walk	440	yds.	(¼ mile)	brisk pace	3:20 min.
	Jog			(2 miles)	walk when necessary	18-24 min.
Day 4	Repeat Day 2					
Day 5	Walk	440	yds.	(¼ mile)	brisk pace	3:20 min.
	Jog	3080	yds.	(1¾ mile)	moderate pace	17:00 min.
	Walk	440	yds.	(¼ mile)	Jog 440 yds.	
	Walk	220	yds.	(⅛ mile)	moderate pace	1:52 min.

WEEK 14

Day 1	Walk	440	yds.	(¼ mile)	brisk pace	3:20 min.
	Jog	440	yds.	(¼ mile)	walk as necessary	2 times
	Jog	220	yds.	(⅛ mile)	walk as necessary	4 times
	Jog	880	yds.	(½ mile)	Walk 220 yds.	

Day 2	Walk	440	yds.	(¼ mile)	brisk pace	3:20 min.
	Jog	3520	yds.	(2 miles)	vary pace	16-23 min.
	Walk	440	yds.	(¼ mile)	moderate pace	3:45 min.
Day 3	Same as Day 1					
Day 4	Walk	440	yds.	(¼ mile)	brisk pace	3:20 min.
	Jog	3520	yds.	(2 miles)	own pace	16-23 min.
	Walk	660	yds.	(⅜ mile)	moderate pace	5:00 min.
Day 5	Repeat Day 4					

WEEK 15

Day 1	Walk	440	yds.	(¼ mile)	brisk pace	3:20 min.
	Jog	3740	yds.	(2⅛ miles)	vary pace	18-25 min.
	Walk	440	yds.	(¼ mile)	moderate pace	3:45 min.
Day 2	Walk	440	yds.	(¼ mile)	brisk pace	3:20 min.
	Jog	3960	yds.	(2¼ miles)	vary pace	19-27 min.
	Walk	220	yds.	(⅛ mile)	moderate pace	1:52 min.
Day 3	Walk	440	yds.	(¼ mile)	brisk pace	3:20 min.
	Jog				at own pace	20:00 min.
	Walk	220	yds.	(⅛ mile)	moderate pace	1:52 min.
Day 4	Walk	440	yds.	(¼ mile)	brisk pace	3:20 min.
	Jog				at own pace, walk if necessary	23:00 min.
	Walk	220	yds.	(⅛ mile)	moderate pace	1:52 min.
Day 5	Walk	440	yds.	(¼ mile)	brisk pace	3:20 min.
	Jog				at own pace	25:00 min.
	Walk	220	yds.	(⅛ mile)	moderate pace	1:52 min.

WEEK 16

Day 1	Walk	440	yds.	(¼ mile)	brisk pace	3:20 min.
	Jog	20	min.		Walk 110 yds.	
	Jog	10	min.		Walk 220 yds.	
Day 2	Walk	440	yds.	(¼ mile)	brisk pace	3:20 min.
	Jog				at own pace	30:00 min.
	Walk	220	yds.	(⅛ mile)	moderate pace	1:52 min.
Day 3	Same as Day 2					
Day 4	Walk	440	yds.	(¼ mile)	brisk pace	3:20 min.
	Jog	1760	yds.	(1 mile)	Walk 110 yds.	
	Jog	1760	yds.	(1 mile)	Walk 220 yds.	
	Jog	1760	yds.	(1 mile)	Walk 440 yds.	
Day 5	Walk	440	yds.	(¼ mile)	brisk pace	3:20 min.
	Jog				at own pace	35:00 min.
	Walk	220	yds.	(⅛ mile)	moderate pace	1:52 min.

APPENDIX B

JOGGING LOG

ame _____ Section _____ Date _____

Date	Resting H.R.	Exercise H.R.	Time	Distance	Total Week	Total Year	Comments

JOGGING LOG

Name _____ Section _____ Date _____

	Date	Resting H.R.	Exercise H.R.	Time	Distance	Total Week	Total Year	Comments
M								
T								
W								
T								
F								
S								
S								
M								
T								
W								
T								
F								
S								
S								
M								
T								
W								
T								
F								
S								
S								

JOGGING LOG

Name _____ Section _____ Date _____

	Date	Resting H.R.	Exercise H.R.	Time	Distance	Total Week	Total Year	Comments
M								
T								
W								
T								
F								
S								
S								
M								
T								
W								
T								
F								
S								
S								
M								
T								
W								
T								
F								
S								
S								

JOGGING LOG

Name _____ Section _____ Date _____

	Date	Resting H.R.	Exercise H.R.	Time	Distance	Total Week	Total Year	Comments
M								
T								
W								
T								
F								
S								
S								
M								
T								
W								
T								
F								
S								
S								
M								
T								
W								
T								
F								
S								
S								

JOGGING LOG

Name _____ Section _____ Date _____

	Date	Resting H.R.	Exercise H.R.	Time	Distance	Total Week	Total Year	Comments
M								
T								
W								
T								
F								
S								
S								
M								
T								
W								
T								
F								
S								
S								
M								
T								
W								
T								
F								
S								
S								

JOGGING LOG

Name _____ Section _____ Date _____

	Date	Resting H.R.	Exercise H.R.	Time	Distance	Total Week	Total Year	Comments
M								
T								
W								
T								
F								
S								
S								
M								
T								
W								
T								
F								
S								
S								
M								
T								
W								
T								
F								
S								
S								

APPENDIX C

ASSESSMENT TESTS, NORMS AND LABORATORY EXERCISES

Laboratory   Page

Laboratory 1

HEART ATTACK RISK FACTORS

Name _____ Section _____ Date _____

Purpose

1. To give you an estimate of your chances of suffering a heart attack.

2. To alert you to certain risk factors in your lifestyle which need to be changed if possible.

Procedure

Following the instructions on the next page, complete the RISKO Scorecard.

	Yourself	Parent
Age		
Heredity		
Weight		
Tobacco Use		
Exercise		
Cholesterol		
Blood Pressure		
Sex		

Results

1. What is your total score? _____ Classification? _____

2. What is the total score for your father or mother? _____
   Classification? _____

RISKO

The purpose of this game is to give you an estimate of your chances of suffering heart attack. The game is played by marking squares which — from left to right — represent an increase in your *risk factors*. These are medical conditions and habits associated with an increased danger of heart attack. Not all risk factors are measurable enough to be included in this game.

Rules: Study each risk factor and its row. Find the box applicable to you and circle the large number in it. For example, if you are age 37, circle the number in the box labeled 31-40.

After checking out all the rows, add the circled numbers. This total — your score — is an estimate of your risk.

If You Score:

6-11 — Risk well below average
12-17 — Risk below average
18-24 — Risk generally average

25-31 — Risk moderate
32-40 — Risk at a dangerous level
41-62 — Danger urgent. See your doctor now.

Heredity: Count parents, grandparents, brothers, and sisters who have had heart attack and/or stroke.

Tobacco Smoking: If you inhale deeply and smoke a cigarette way down, add one to your classification. Do *not* subtract because you think you do not inhale or smoke only a half inch on a cigarette.

Exercise: Lower your score one point if you exercise regularly and frequently.

Cholesterol or Saturated Fat Intake Level: A cholesterol blood level is best. If you can't get one from your doctor, then estimate honestly the percentage of solid fats you eat. These are usually of animal origin — lard, cream, butter, and beef and lamb fat. If you eat much of this, your cholesterol level probably will be high. The United States average, 40 percent, is too high for good health.

Blood Pressure: If you have no recent reading but have passed an insurance or industrial examination chances are you are 140 or less.

Sex: This line takes into account the fact that men have from 6 to 10 times more heart attacks than women of child bearing age.

Conclusions and Implications

1. What areas of risk represent your greatest problem?

2. What areas of risk represent your mother or father's greatest problem?

3. What areas of risk would be your greatest problem in the future?

Lab 1, *continued*

Name _____ Section _____ Date _____

AGE	10 to 20	21 to 30	31 to 40	41 to 50	51 to 60	61 to 70
HEREDITY	No known history of heart disease	1 relative with cardiovascular disease Over 60	2 relatives with cardiovascular disease Over 60	1 relative with cardiovascular disease Under 60	2 relatives with cardiovascular disease Under 60	3 relatives with cardiovascular disease Under 60
WEIGHT	More than 5 lbs. below standard weight	−5 to + 5 lbs standard weight	6-20 lbs over weight	21-35 lbs over weight	36-50 lbs over weight	51-65 lbs over weight
TOBACCO SMOKING	Non-user	Cigar and/or pipe	10 cigarettes or less a day	20 cigarettes a day	30 cigarettes a day	40 cigarettes a day or more
EXERCISE	Intensive occupational and recreational exertion	Moderate occupational and recreational exertion	Sedentary work and intense recreational exertion	Sedentary occupational and moderate exertion	Sedentary work and light recreational	Complete lack of all exercise
CHOLES-TEROL OR FAT % IN DIET	Cholesterol below 180 mg % Diet contains no animal or solid fats	Cholesterol 181-205 mg % Diet contains 10% animal or solid fats	Cholesterol 206-230 mg % Diet contains 20% animal or solid fats	Cholesterol 231-255 mg % Diet contains 30% animal or solid fats	Cholesterol 256-280 mg % Diet contains 40% animal or solid fats	Cholesterol 281-300 mg % Diet contains 50% animal or solid fats
BLOOD PRESSURE	100 upper reading	120 upper reading	140 upper reading	160 upper reading	180 upper reading	200 or over upper reading
SEX	Female under 40	Female 40-50	Female over 50	Male	Stocky male	Bald stocky male

Reprinted through the courtesy of the Michigan Heart Association. Copyright © Michigan Heart Association.

For meaningful interpretation of RISKO only the official RISKO directions should be used.

Conclusions and Implications, *continued*

4. What specific steps can you take to reduce your risks?

Laboratory 2

SHOE ASSESSMENT

Name _____ Section _____ Date _____

Purpose

1. To assist in identifying individual footwear needs.
2. To acquaint you with shoe brands that may satisfy these needs.

Procedure

1. Read Chapter 7 and then consider the points listed below under results.
2. Inspect your old shoes for unusual wear characteristics.

Results

1. What individual needs have you identified in the selection of running shoes?
   1. Foot shape
   2. Foot structure characteristics
   3. Foot size
   4. Body weight
   5. Present level of physical activity
   6. Running surface
   7. Running style

2. Visit the library and review the annual shoe issue of *Runner's World* magazine. Select a number of shoe brands that rated high in areas you feel are important to meet your individual needs.

Conclusions and Implications

1. Have you owned a pair of jogging shoes previously? How do you evaluate their wear characteristics?

2. What brand and style of jogging shoe do you feel will best meet your needs?

Item	Shoe Brand			
Suggested Retail Price				
Test Results* 1. Flexibility				
2. Rearfoot Impact				
3. Forefoot Impact				
4. Sole Wear				
5. Rearfoot Control				
6. Sole Traction				
Upper Information				
Soles				
General Information				

*Note: Test results one through six correspond with tests conducted by *Runner's World*.

Laboratory 3

DESIGNING YOUR WARM-UP AND COOL-DOWN SESSIONS

Name _____ Section _____ Date _____

Purpose

1. To assist in recognizing the importance of a warm-up and cool-down period.
2. To aid in the selection of activities designed for pre and post exercise sessions.
3. To provide an opportunity to practice stretching exercises.

Procedure

1. Read Chapter 5 regarding principles underlying the warm-up and cool-down session.
2. Why is the warm-up essential to a jogging program?

3. What is the importance of the cool-down?

4. Identify areas of muscle soreness experienced in past exercise sessions.

5. Perform stretching exercises illustrated in Chapter 5.
6. Begin walking and progress into a slow jog. Keep increasing pace until target zone is reached. Gradually, slow pace until heart rate drops to 120 beats per minute. Perform some of the same pre-activity stretching exercises until heart rate drops to within normal range.

Results

1. Were you able to identify exercises that stretched muscles that have given you problems in the past?

2. How many minutes did it take for your total warm-up (from normal heart rate to target zone)?

3. How many minutes did it take to cool down?

Conclusions and Implications

1. Do you feel more like jogging after a proper warm-up?

2. Do you notice a difference in how you feel if you cool down properly after activity in comparison to how you feel if the cool-down is neglected?

   a. Immediately:

   b. Six hours later:

   c. Next day:

3. Design a warm-up and cool-down program to fit your individual needs.

Laboratory 4

COMPUTATION OF BODY COMPOSITION

Name _____ Section _____ Date _____

Purpose

1. To assess percentage of body fat.
2. To assist in determining optimal body weight.
3. To acquaint you with a method of determining optimal body weight which can be utilized throughout life.
4. To become aware of the difference between overweight and obesity.

Procedure

1. Determine current body weight.
2. Stand with right side next to person taking measurements.
   a. Measurements are taken for the following areas of the body:
      Triceps — midpoint between the shoulder and elbow on the posterior (back) of the arm.
      Subscapula — below the shoulder blade.
   b. Measurement is made by pinching a fold of skin between the thumb and forefinger, pulling the fold away from the underlying muscle and applying the caliper to the fold. An average of two to three consecutive measurements at each site should be obtained.
3. Record the measurement to the nearest millimeter, using the mean of the two readings.
4. Compute lean body weight, percent fat, and ideal body weight using formula on next page.

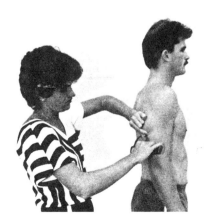 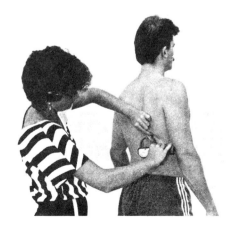

Results

1. Readings:

	1st	2nd	3rd	Average
a. Tricep skinfold	_____	_____	_____	_____
b. Subscapula	_____	_____	_____	_____

2. What is your mean skinfold measurement? $(a + b) \div 2 =$ _____

3. What is your actual body weight? _____

4. What is your desired weight as determined from the height-weight chart in Chapter 10?_____

5. What is your lean body weight?_____

6. What is your relative percent of fat?_____

7. What is your ideal body weight?_____

8. How many pounds are you currently under or over weight?_____

Conclusions and Implications

1. How does your ideal body weight compare with your desired weight as determined from the height-weight chart?

2. Do you feel that this calculation reflects a realistic ideal weight for you?

3. What implications do these results have for your diet and exercise plans?

FITNESS CATEGORY	BODY FAT PERCENTAGE (1)	
	PERCENT FAT	CATEGORY
	male	female
Very Lean	10%	13%
Lean	11-15%	14-18%
Average	16-19%	19-22%
Fat	20-24%	23-27%
Very Fat	25%	28%

COMPUTATION OF BODY COMPOSITION — MEN

MEN — LEAN BODY WEIGHT

A. Put down 22.62 _____ A. _____

B. Multiply .793 × **your body weight** _____ B. _____

C. Add **A** and **B** _____ C. _____

D. Multiply your skinfold of ____ × .801 _____ D. _____

E. Subtract **D** from **C** above _____ E. _____

The figure you have in **E** is your **LEAN BODY WEIGHT.**

MEN — RELATIVE PERCENT (%) OF FAT

A. Put down your body weight _____ A. _____

B. Record your *lean body weight* (E above) _____ B. _____

C. Subtract **B** from **A** _____ C. _____

D. Divide your weight into **C** _____ D. _____

E. Multiply line **D** × 100 _____ E. _____

The figure you have on line **E** is your PERCENTAGE (%) OF FAT

MEN — IDEAL BODY WEIGHT

A. Put down your *lean body weight* _____ A. _____

B. Divide .85 into **A** _____ B. _____

The figure you have on line **B** is your **IDEAL BODY WEIGHT** AT THIS TIME.

COMPUTATION OF BODY COMPOSITION — WOMEN

WOMEN — LEAN BODY WEIGHT

A. Put down 20.20 _____ A. _____20.20_____

B. Multiply .635 × **your body weight** _____ B. _____

C. Add **A** and **B** _____ C. _____

D. Multiply your skinfold of ____ × .503 _____ D. _____

E. Subtract **D** from **C** above _____ E. _____

The figure you have in **E** is your **LEAN BODY WEIGHT.**

WOMEN — RELATIVE PERCENTAGE (%) OF FAT

A. Put down your body weight _____ A. _____

B. Record your *lean body weight* (E above) _____ B. _____

C. Subtract **B** from **A** _____ C. _____

D. Divide your weight into **C** _____ D. _____

E. Multiply line **D** × 100 _____ E. _____

The figure you have in **E** is your **PERCENTAGE (%) OF FAT.**

WOMEN — IDEAL BODY WEIGHT

A. Put down your *lean body weight* _____ A. _____

B. Divide .775 into **A** _____ B. _____

The figure you have on line **B** is your **IDEAL BODY WEIGHT** AT THIS TIME.

Laboratory 5

LUNG CAPACITY ASSESSMENT

Name _____ Section _____ Date _____

Vital lung capacity is a measurement of the maximum amount of air that can be expired after a maximum inspiration.

Purpose

1. To assist in determining the condition of your lungs.
2. To determine whether an airway obstruction is present.

Procedure

The test is performed by having the subject stand erect and inhale as deeply as possible. Place mouthpiece of spirometer in mouth so that lips form a good air seal. Then exhale forcefully and completely.

Results

1. What was your score in liters for vital lung capacity?

   pre-test? _____   post-test? _____

2. What was your classification?

   pre-test? _____   post-test? _____

Conclusions and Implications

An average adult lung holds approximately 6,200 to 7,400 milliliters of air, depending on body size (Dimensions). About 1,200 milliliters of residual air is never expelled. Thus the maximum amount of air that can be expired after vital capacity (maximum inspiration) is approximately 4,500 to 6,000 milliliters for males and 3,000 to 4,500 milliliters for females.

A. 1. If your capacity is low what do you think the reason is?

    2. What specific steps can be taken to increase your vital capacity?

B. 1. How do the results of the pre-test compare with the post test?

    2. What specific steps can be taken to increase your classification?

FITNESS	LUNG CAPACITY (DRY) ASSESSMENT SCORES	
	male	female
Excellent	>5500	>4000
Good	4700-5400	3600-3900
Average	3900-4600	2800-3500
Poor	3100-3800	2100-2700
Very Poor	<3000	<2000

VITAL CAPACITY
(Wet Spirometer)

Classifi-cation	T	%	Vital Capacity male	Vital Capacity female	Classifi-cation	T	%	Vital Capacity male	Vital Capacity female
A	80	99.9	6.6	4.8	C	49	46.0	4.3	
A	79	99.8	6.5	4.7	C	48	42.1	4.2	
A	78	99.7	6.4	4.6	C	47	38.2	4.1	2.9
A	77	99.6	6.3	4.5	C	46	34.5		2.8
A	76	99.5			C	45	30.8	4.0	2.7
A	75	99.4	6.2	4.4	D	44	27.4	3.9	
A	74	99.2	6.1	4.3	D	43	24.2		
A	73	98.9			D	42	21.2	3.8	
A	72	98.6	6.0		D	41	18.4		
A	71	98.2	5.9	4.2	D	40	15.9	3.7	2.5
A	70	97.7	5.8	4.1	D	39	13.6	3.6	
A	69	97.1			D	38	11.5	3.5	2.4
A	68	96.8	5.7	4.0	D	37	9.7	3.4	
A	67	95.5	5.6		D	36	8.1		2.3
A	66	94.5		3.9	D	35	6.7	3.3	2.2
A	65	93.9	5.5	3.8	E	34	5.5	3.2	
B	64	92.6			E	33	4.5	3.1	
B	63	90.3	5.4		E	32	3.6	3.0	2.1'
B	62	88.5	5.3	3.7	E	31	2.9		2.0
B	61	86.4	5.2		E	30	2.3	2.9	1.9

Continued on next page

VITAL CAPACITY, Continued
(Wet Spirometer)

Classifi-cation	T	%	Vital Capacity male	Vital Capacity female	Classifi-cation	T	%	Vital Capacity male	Vital Capacity female
B	60	84.1	5.1		E	29	1.8		1.8
B	59	81.6		3.6	E	28	1.4	2.8	
B	58	78.8	5.0	3.5	E	27	1.1	2.7	1.7
B	57	75.8			E	26	0.8		
B	56	72.6	4.9	3.4	E	25	0.6	2.6	1.6
B	55	69.2	4.8	3.3	E	24	0.5	2.5	
C	54	65.5	4.7		E	23	0.4	2.4	1.5
C	53	61.8	4.6	3.2	E	22	0.3	2.3	
C	52	57.9			E	21	0.2	2.2	
C	51	54.0	4.5	3.1	E	20	0.1	2.1	1.4
C	50	50.0	4.4	3.0					

Laboratory 6

SIT AND STAND HEART RATE RECOVERY TEST

Name _____ Section _____ Date _____

This exercise is a relatively simple test of sitting and standing 24 times a minute for 3 minutes. Since the test is not as strenuous as a step test, it is relatively safe to administer as a basic screening test for cardiovascular health. The results enable one to determine the general fitness zone: danger zone, safety zone, or fitness zone.

Purpose

1. To assist in evaluating cardiovascular efficiency by means of a sit and stand test.
2. To provide an effective method of evaluating your cardiovascular fitness throughout life.

Procedure

1. Preliminary procedure
   a. Sit in a chair for at least 10 minutes.
   b. Assistant counts pretest pulse rate for 15 seconds and multiplies by 4.
2. Action
   Starting from a sitting position with arms folded, stand up and sit down twice every 5 seconds (24 times a minute) for 3 minutes.
3. Post-Action Activity
   a. Immediately sit down and find your pulse. Count pulse for 15 seconds and record it as the Immediate Post Test Heart Rate Index.
   b. The 30-Second Recovery Heart Rate is recorded after taking the pulse once again for 15 seconds (from 30 seconds after the exercise bout to 45 seconds after it).
   c. The One-Minute and Two-Minute Recovery Heart Rate is recorded in a similar manner.
   d. Multiply the post-test heart rate and all recovery heart rate scores by 4.

Results

1. On the chart provided, circle the heart rate scores for the test and find the codes directly above the circled heart rates. Write the codes in the space provided to the right of the chart.
2. Add the codes for all five heart rates and circle the total code score which indicates your fitness zone.

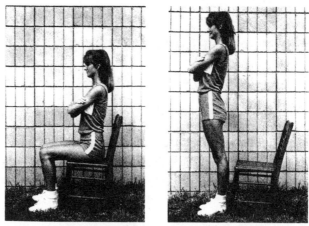

HEART RATE RECOVERY (SIT/STAND TEST)

CODING YOUR CARDIOVASCULAR HEALTH CODES

Code Score

	20	19	18	17	16	15	14	13	12	11	10	9	8	7	6	5	4	3	2	1	
Starting Heart Rate	44	48	52	56	60	62	64	66	68	70	72	74	76	78	80	84	88	92	96	100	___
Post test Heart Rate	80	84	88	92	96	100	104	108	112	116	120	124	128	132	136	140	144	148	152	156	___
30-Second Recovery Heart Rate	64	68	72	76	80	84	88	92	96	100	104	108	112	116	120	124	128	132	136	140	___
1-Minute Recovery Heart Rate	56	60	64	68	72	76	80	84	88	92	96	100	104	108	112	116	120	124	128	132	___
2-Minute Recovery Heart Rate	56	60	64	68	72	76	80	84	88	92	96	100	104	108	112	116	120	124	128	132	___

Results

0-35 = Danger Zone
36-70 = Safety Zone
71-100 = Fitness Zone

Total Code Scores

=====

Conclusions and Implications

1. Are you pleased or displeased with your score?

2. In twenty years at your present level of physical activity, what zone do you think you would fall in?

Laboratory 7

HARVARD STEP TEST

Name _____ Section _____ Date _____

The Harvard Step Test was developed at Harvard University Fatigue Laboratories as an easily administered measure of cardiovascular endurance. The test is based upon the premise that for a given work task, the person with a higher level of cardiovascular fitness will have a smaller increase in heart rate, and that following the task, heart rate will return to normal much faster than for a person who has a lower level of cardiovascular fitness.

Purpose:

1. To assist in evaluating your cardiovascular fitness level by means of a step test.
2. To acquaint you with effective methods of evaluating your cardiovascular fitness throughout life.

Procedure

1. Preparatory procedure
   a. Assistant counts and records pretest pulse rate for 30 seconds.
   b. Starting position: stand erect facing side of box at a comfortable stepping distance.
   c. Height of box for males — 20 inches; for females — 16 inches.
2. Action (begin on starting signal)
   a. Step up onto the box with first one foot and then the other, assuming a momentary straight stand.
   b. Immediately step down to the starting position.
   c. Repeat continuously until the signal to stop is given.
   d. Rate of stepping: thirty times per minutes; i.e., one complete sequence every two seconds. Continue activity for a period of five minutes, or until unable to continue at prescribed rate.
3. Post-Action Activity
   a. Immediately sit down and rest.
   b. After cessation of exercise, assistant counts pulse for 30 seconds, at one minute, two minute, and three minute intervals.
   c. Record the sum of the three pulse counts.
   d. Refer to scoring table.

The test is scored by counting the recovery pulse rate after one minute, two minutes, and three minutes of rest.

Results

1. What was your pulse at each recovery period?

   one minute _____   two minutes _____   three minutes _____

   Sum of three pulse counts _____

2. What was your fitness classification? _____

Conclusions and Implications

1. How does this test compare to other measures of cardiovascular fitness?

2. Which cardiovascular test seemed the most difficult for you to complete? Why?

3. Have you seen improvement in your fitness classification since your last test of cardiovascular fitness?

HARVARD STEP TEST
5 Minute Duration

CLASSI-FICATION	T	%	SUM OF 3 PULSE COUNTS FEMALE	MALE		CLASSI-FICATION	T	%	SUM OF 3 PULSE COUNTS FEMALE	MALE
A+	80	99.9	103-101	101		C	49	46.0	176-175	177-176
A+	79	99.8	105-104	104-103		C	48	42.1	179-177	180-178
A	78	99.7	107-106	106-105		C	47	38.2	181-180	182-181
A	77	99.6	108	108-107		C	46	34.5	184-182	184-183
A	76	99.5	111-109	111-109		C	45	30.8	186-185	187-185
A	75	99.4	113-112	113-112		D+	44	27.4	189-187	189-188
A	74	99.2	116-114	116-114		D+	43	24.2	191-190	192-190
A	73	98.9	118-117	118-117		D+	42	21.2	194-192	195-193
A	72	98.6	120-119	121-119		D+	41	18.4	196-195	197-196
A	71	98.2	123-121	123-122		D+	40	15.9	198-197	199-198
A	70	97.7	125-124	126-124		D	39	13.6	201-199	202-200
A	69	97.1	128-126	128-127		D	38	11.5	203-202	204-203
A	68	96.8	130-129	131-129		D	37	9.7	206-204	207-205
A	67	95.5	133-131	133-132		D	36	8.1	208-207	209-208
A	66	94.5	135-134	135-134		D	35	6.7	211-209	211-210
A	65	93.9	137-136	138-136		E+	34	5.5	213-212	214-212
B+	64	92.6	140-138	140-139		E+	33	4.5	215-214	216-215
B+	63	90.3	142-141	143-141		E+	32	3.6	218-216	219-217
B+	62	88.5	145-143	145-144		E+	31	2.9	220-219	221-220
B+	61	86.4	147-146	148-146		E+	30	2.3	223-221	224-222
B+	60	84.1	150-148	150-149		E	29	1.8	225-224	226-225
B	59	81.6	152-151	153-151		E	28	1.4	228-226	229-227
B	58	78.8	155-153	155-152		E	27	1.1	230-229	231-230
B	57	75.8	157-156	158-156		E	26	0.8	233-231	233-232
B	56	72.6	159-158	160-159		E	25	0.6	235-234	236-234
B	55	69.2	162-160	162-161		E	24	0.5	237-236	238-237
C+	54	65.5	164-163	165-163		E	23	0.4	240-238	241-239
C+	53	61.8	167-165	167-164		E	22	0.3	242-241	243-240
C+	52	57.9	160-168	170-168		E	21	0.2	245-243	246-242
C+	51	54.0	172-170	172-171		E	20	0.1	247-246	248-245
C+	50	50.0	174-173	175-173						

Laboratory 8

12 - MINUTE RUN/WALK TEST

Name _____ Section _____ Date _____

This simple test of working capacity correlates well with laboratory measurements such as the bicycle ergometer. The test, developed by Dr. Kenneth Cooper, measures the distance covered within the allotted time. By evaluating the distance covered, one can be rated in terms of maximum oxygen consumption.

Purpose

1. To assist in evaluating your cardiovascular fitness level.
2. To provide an effective means of evaluating your cardiovascular fitness throughout life.

Procedure

1. Warm up following suggestions in Chapter 5.
2. Start the timer and cover as much distance as possible by running, jogging or walking in the allotted 12-minute period.
3. Cool down by following suggestions in Chapter 5.
4. Record the distance covered.

Results

1. What distance did you complete in the 12 minutes?

   Pre-Test _____   Post Test _____
2. What is your rating? Pre-test _____ Post Test _____

Conclusions and Implications

1. Did you score as well as you thought you would?

2. Were you able to maintain a steady pace throughout the 12 minutes?

3. Do you feel this test reflects your true cardiovascular fitness level?

TWELVE MINUTE RUN/WALK

CLASSIFICATION	T	%	MALE LAPS	FEMALE LAPS
A+	80	99.9	9	8
A+	79	99.8		$7\tfrac{7}{8}$
A	78	99.7	$8\tfrac{7}{8}$	$7\tfrac{6}{8}$
A	77	99.6	$8\tfrac{6}{8}$	$7\tfrac{5}{8}$
A	76	99.5	$8\tfrac{5}{8}$	$7\tfrac{4}{8}$
A	75	99.4	$8\tfrac{4}{8}$	$7\tfrac{3}{8}$
A	74	99.2		$7\tfrac{2}{8}$
A	73	98.9	$8\tfrac{3}{8}$	$7\tfrac{1}{8}$
A	72	98.6	$8\tfrac{2}{8}$	7
A	71	98.2		$6\tfrac{7}{8}$
A	70	97.7	$8\tfrac{1}{8}$	
A	69	97.1		$6\tfrac{6}{8}$
A	68	96.8	8	
A	67	95.5	$7\tfrac{7}{8}$	$6\tfrac{5}{8}$
A	66	94.5		$6\tfrac{4}{8}$
A	65	93.9	$7\tfrac{6}{8}$	$6\tfrac{3}{8}$
B+	64	92.6		$6\tfrac{2}{8}$
B+	63	90.3	$7\tfrac{5}{8}$	
B+	62	88.5		$6\tfrac{1}{8}$
B+	61	86.4	$7\tfrac{4}{8}$	6
B+	60	84.1		
B	59	81.6	$7\tfrac{3}{8}$	
B	58	78.8		$5\tfrac{7}{8}$
B	57	75.8	$7\tfrac{2}{8}$	$5\tfrac{6}{8}$
B	56	72.6		$5\tfrac{5}{8}$
B	55	69.2	$7\tfrac{1}{8}$	$5\tfrac{4}{8}$
C+	54	65.5		
C+	53	61.8	7	$5\tfrac{3}{8}$
C+	52	57.9		
C+	51	54.0	$6\tfrac{7}{8}$	$5\tfrac{2}{8}$
C+	50	50.0		

CLASSIFICATION	T	%	MALE LAPS	FEMALE LAPS
C	49	46.0	$6\tfrac{6}{8}$	$5\tfrac{1}{8}$
C	48	42.1		5
C	47	38.2	$6\tfrac{5}{8}$	
C	46	34.5	$6\tfrac{4}{8}$	
C	45	30.8		
D+	44	27.4	$6\tfrac{3}{8}$	$4\tfrac{7}{8}$
D+	43	24.2	$6\tfrac{2}{8}$	$4\tfrac{6}{8}$
D+	42	21.2		$4\tfrac{5}{8}$
D+	41	18.4	$6\tfrac{1}{8}$	
D	40	15.9		$4\tfrac{4}{8}$
D	39	13.6	6	
D	38	11.5	$5\tfrac{7}{8}$	$4\tfrac{3}{8}$
D	37	9.7	$5\tfrac{6}{8}$	
D	36	8.1	$5\tfrac{5}{8}$	$4\tfrac{2}{8}$
D	35	6.7	$5\tfrac{4}{8}$	$4\tfrac{1}{8}$
E+	34	5.5	$5\tfrac{3}{8}$	4
E+	33	4.5	$5\tfrac{2}{8}$	
E+	32	3.6	$5\tfrac{1}{8}$	$3\tfrac{7}{8}$
E+	31	2.9	5	$3\tfrac{6}{8}$
E	30	2.3	$4\tfrac{7}{8}$	$3\tfrac{5}{8}$
E	29	1.8	$4\tfrac{6}{8}$	$3\tfrac{4}{8}$
E	28	1.4	$4\tfrac{5}{8}$	$3\tfrac{3}{8}$
E	27	1.2	$4\tfrac{4}{8}$	
E	26	0.8	$4\tfrac{3}{8}$	$3\tfrac{2}{8}$
E	25	0.6	$4\tfrac{2}{8}$	
E	24	0.5	$4\tfrac{1}{8}$	$3\tfrac{1}{8}$
E	23	0.4	4	
E	22	0.3	$3\tfrac{7}{8}$	3
E	21	0.2	$3\tfrac{6}{8}$	$2\tfrac{7}{8}$
E	20	0.1	$3\tfrac{5}{8}$	$2\tfrac{4}{8}$

4. What implications do the test results have for your exercise needs?

Laboratory 9

1.5 MILE RUN TEST

Name _____ Section _____ Date _____

The 1.5 mile run test is an alternate method of field testing which correlates well with one's maximum oxygen consumption determined from laboratory results.

Purpose

1. To provide an effective means of evaluating your present cardiovascular fitness level.
2. To acquaint you with an effective means of evaluating your cardiovascular fitness throughout life.

Procedure

1. Warm up by following suggestions in Chapter 5.
2. Start the timer and cover the required distance (1.5 miles) by running, jogging, or walking.
3. After traveling 1.5 miles, stop the timer and record the time to nearest second.
4. Cool down by following suggestions in Chapter 5.

Results

1. How much time did it take for you to run the 1.5 miles? _____

2. What is your cardiovascular fitness rating? _____

Conclusions and Implications

1. Did you score as well as you thought you would?

2. Were you able to maintain a steady pace throughout the 1.5 mile distance?

3. Do you feel this test indicates your true cardiovascular fitness level?

4. What implications does the test have for your exercise needs?

1.5 MILE RUN

MALES (BY AGE)

FITNESS CATEGORY	13-19	20-29	30-39	40-49	50-59	60 +
Superior	<8:37	<9:45	<10:00	<10:30	<11:00	<11:15
Excellent	8:37-9:40	9:45-10:45	10:00-11:00	10:30-11:30	11:00-12:30	11:15-13:59
Good	9:41-10:48	10:46-12:00	11:01-12:30	11:31-13:00	12:31-14:30	14:00-16:15
Fair	10:49-12:10	12:01-14:00	12:31-14:45	13:01-15:35	14:31-17:00	16:16-19:00
Poor	12:11-15:30	14:01-16:00	14:46-16:30	15:36-17:30	17:01-19:00	19:01-20:00
Very Poor	>15:31	>16:10	>16:31	>17:31	>19:01	>20:01

1.5 MILE RUN

FEMALES (BY AGE)

FITNESS CATEGORY	13-19	20-29	30-39	40-49	50-59	60 +
Superior	>11:50	>12:30	>13:00	>13:45	>14:30	>16:30
Excellent	11:50-12:29	12:30-13:30	13:00-14:30	13:45-15:55	14:30-16:30	16:30-17:30
Good	12:30-14:3C	13:31-15:54	14:31-16:30	15:56-17:30	16:31-19:00	17:31-19:30
Fair	14:31-16:54	15:55-18:30	16:31-19:00	17:31-19:30	19:01-20:00	19:31-20:30
Poor	16:55-18:30	18:31-19:00	19:01-19:30	19:31-20:00	20:01-20:30	20:31-21:00
Very Poor	<18:31	<19:01	<19:31	<20:01	<20:31	<21:01

$>$ = more than　　$<$ = less than

Laboratory 10

BLOOD PRESSURE RECOVERY

Name _____ Section _____ Date _____

Purpose

To determine the effect of exercise on your blood pressure and to see how quickly your blood pressure returns to the starting level.

Procedure

1. Assume a sitting position for 5 minutes. Measure blood pressure and record.
2. Jog until the 70 percent target heart rate is reached.
3. Stop exercising and again assume a sitting position. Partner will determine blood pressure immediately following the exercise bout.
4. Partner will continue to take blood pressure and record until it returns to the starting rate.

Starting Blood Pressure _____

70% Training Heart Rate _____

Exercise Blood Pressure _____

Recovery Blood Pressure _____

1 minute _____

3 minutes _____

5 minutes _____

10 minutes _____

Conclusions and Implications

1. What do the results of the lab indicate in regard to your blood pres-

   sure: before exercise _____

   _____ immediately after exercise _____

   _____

   recovery rate after exercise _____

   _____

2. What other factors besides exercise might cause your blood pressure values
   to change?

3. How does the well-trained individual's blood pressure respond during exercise?

Laboratory 11

ANALYZING JOGGING FORM

Name _____ Section _____ Date _____

Purpose

Although there is no single correct way to jog, the purpose of this session is to provide you with feedback that may prevent injuries and allow you to be more energy efficient.

Procedures

1. Read Chapter 6 before you continue with this lab session.
2. As you are performing one of the cardiovascular assessment tests or while jogging, have someone complete the following check list.

	YES	NO
a. Runs erect and tall	_____	_____
b. Head is up, with eyes looking straight ahead	_____	_____
c. Swing legs from hip with bent knees	_____	_____
d. Lands on heel, allowing weight to roll along outside edge of foot to toes	_____	_____
e. Heel contacts ground directly under knee	_____	_____
f. Toes are pointed straight ahead	_____	_____
g. Arms and hands are relaxed, swinging forward easily	_____	_____
h. Breathing is abdominal and in rhythm.	_____	_____

Results

1. How many items were checked yes?

2. What items were checked no?

Conclusions and Implications

1. Do you feel those items checked "no" will cause you displeasure or injury?

2. What items do you wish to improve?

3. How do you feel about your jogging form?

Laboratory 12

TARGET HEART RATE ZONE

Name _____ Section _____ Date _____

Target heart rate zone identifies the safe and comfortable pace that should be maintained to achieve a training effect.

Purpose

1. To assist in determining your present target heart rate zone.
2. To acquaint you with a method which can be used throughout your life to determine the target zone.

Procedures

		Example

1. Determine your maximum heart rate according to your age.   220   220

   220 − age = maximum heart rate

   − _____ − 20

2. Determine your resting heart rate by method described = _____ = 200 in Chapter 2 and subtract it from step 1.

   − _____ − 70

3. Determine at what percent overload you desire to train. = _____ = 130 The safe upper limit is 85% and the lower limit is 70% for training effect.

   × _____ × .70

4. Multiply step 3 times the value of step 2. = _____ = 91
5. Add the resting heart rate. + _____ + 70
6. Lower limit of target heart rate for training effect. = _____ = 161

Results

1. Using the formula described above and presented below, complete your target heart rate for 50%, 60%, 70%, and 85% limits.

   220 − age − resting pulse × % + resting pulse = target zone

   50% = _____ ÷ 6 = _____   70% = _____ ÷ 6 = _____

   60% = _____ ÷ 6 = _____   85% = _____ ÷ 6 = _____

2. Divide the above target zones by six. This will provide you with an instant indication of your target zone. (10 second count)

3. Take your pulse for 10 seconds after walking, jogging and running.

Conclusions and Implications

1. Why is age a factor in determining your target heart rate?

2. Why is the resting heart rate taken into consideration?

3. Why is it necessary to elevate your heart rate above the normal rate while exercising?

4. Should the training ever be started at a level lower than 70%?

5. Is it ever acceptable to exercise above the 85% limit?

Laboratory 13

DESIGNING A PERSONALIZED JOGGING PROGRAM

Name _____ Section _____ Date _____

Purpose

1. To provide the necessary concepts for the development of a jogging program.

2. To create an opportunity to experience a jogging program designed specifically for your individual needs.

Procedure

1. Based upon data below select overload percent and compute target heart rate.

   a. Age _____, Resting HR _____, Blood Pressure _____

   b. Cardiovascular assessment _____ Classification _____

   c. Previous level of physical activity _____

   d. Training heart rate _____ percent = _____ target zone

2. Determine fitness goal:

3. Following the recommended guidelines in Chapter 4, jog for one week to determine appropriate starting point for you.

Results

1. Complete the following after each day's work out.

	Day						
	1	2	3	4	5	6	7
Frequency (check days involved)	___	___	___	___	___	___	___
Duration (minutes involved)	___	___	___	___	___	___	___
Intensity (heart rate while jogging)	___	___	___	___	___	___	___
Recovery Heart Rate							
a. 5 minutes after	___	___	___	___	___	___	___
b. 10 minutes after	___	___	___	___	___	___	___

2. Did you alternate walking with jogging, or were you able to maintain the same pace throughout each program?

Conclusions and Implications

1. Have you ever participated in a jogging program?

2. Did you increase or decrease overload? How?
   a. Intensity

   b. Duration

   c. Frequency

3. Based on the above information, design a personal jogging program applying the overload principle with established goals for each week.

Week	Distance	Time	Freq./wk.
1.			
2.			
3.			
4.			
5.			
6.			
7.			
8.			
9.			
10.			
11.			
12.			
13.			
14.			
15.			
16.			

Laboratory 14

INTERVAL TRAINING

Name _____ Section _____ Date _____

Purpose

The purpose of this session is to provide an opportunity to develop cardiovascular fitness through the use of an interval training program.

Procedure

Read Chapter 4 which describes an interval program and then perform the series of exercises which are listed below.

1. Warm up by doing five minutes of stretching exercises.

2. Take pulse for ten seconds and multiply by 6. Compare with resting pulse.

3. Walk fast around track.

4. Take pulse and compare with pre-activity.

5. Jog one lap slowly.

6. Take pulse and compare.

7. Run 220 yards.

8. Take pulse and compare.

9. *First work session*: Jog for three minutes at a pace that will maintain heart rate in target zone.

10. Take pulse and compare.

11. Walk until heart rate drops to 120 or for three minutes, whichever comes first.

12. *Second work session*: Jog for three minutes.

13. Take pulse and compare.

14. Walk until heart rate drops to 120 or for three minutes, whichever comes first.

15. *Third work session*: Jog for three minutes.

16. Take pulse and compare.

17. Walk until heart rate drops to 120 or for three minutes, whichever comes first.

18. Complete warm-down by doing stretching exercises.

Results

1. Were you able to find and maintain a pace that kept your heart rate in the target zone?

2. Did you reach your target zone on all three work sessions?

3. How long did it take for your heart to recover to 120 beats per minute after a work session?

4. Which work session produced the highest heart rate? Why?

Conclusions and Implications

1. Do you consider this a desirable form of cardiovascular training? Why or why not?

2. How could the overload principle be applied to interval training?

3. Would you be likely to include this type of workout in your exercise program? Why or why not?

Laboratory 15

SELECTION OF A JOGGING ROUTE

Name _____ Section _____ Date _____

Purpose

To provide criteria for selecting a jogging course.

Procedure

1. Using criteria in Chapter 9 select a jogging course.
2. Draw the jogging course on the page supplied.
   a. Measure the distance and indicate each ¼ mile on map.
   b. Note danger points on map (i.e., wet places, loose rock, etc.).

Results

1. What is the total distance of your route?

2. What type of surface(s) does it have?

3. What type of environment classification is it?

4. What is the course layout?

Conclusions and Implications

1. What are the advantages of your course?

2. What are the disadvantages and/or safety considerations for your course?

3. How does this course meet your individual needs?

Scale

Laboratory 16

JOGGING LOG SUMMARY

Name _____ Section _____ Date _____

Purpose

1. To assist in evaluating your personal jogging program.
2. To aid in recognizing the importance of objective data in planning stages of progression.

Procedure

Following instructions in Appendix B, log each workout session.

Results

1. Compute data summary:
   a. Total number of days involved in program   _____
   b. Total number of miles jogged during program   _____
   c. Number of days actually jogged   _____
   d. Number of days you did not jog (a − c)   _____
   e. Percent of days jogged (c ÷ a)   _____
   f. Percent of days you did not jog (d ÷ a)   _____
   g. Average miles per jogging day (b ÷ c)   _____
   h. Average miles for all days involved (b ÷ a)   _____

2. Draw line graph of miles jogged per week.

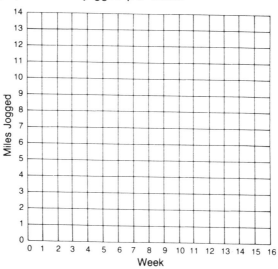

Conclusions and Implications

Write a one-page summary of your experience, describing feelings, changed attitudes, or unusual experiences.